WTF, GOD?

Understanding God in the Midst of Transition

Michelle N. Onuorah

WTF, God?: Understanding God in the Midst of Transition
Published by MNO Media, LLC
Printed in the U.S.A.

ISBN-13: 978-0996627115
ISBN-10: 0996627111

Other Titles by
Michelle N. Onuorah

This book is dedicated to my beloved
grandmother and lifelong friend:

Her Royal Highness, Princess Florence Grace Moradeke
Oshodi, known to me simply as "Ma."

Ma, thank you for your never-ending love, your fountain of
strength, your relentless and tenacious display of faith in God.
I am so proud of you not only for all you've done and how
you've grown but for *who you are.* You are a warrior. You are a
survivor. You are a champion. And you are deeply, *deeply*
loved. Everyone, even strangers, likes you because you are
simply a fantastic human being. I hope to one day be as loving
and generous a woman as you have been your entire life. May
God grant us many more years together. I love you dearly,
Ma, and cherish being your granddaughter.

WTF, GOD?

Contents

FOREWORD

When I was twenty-two years old, my world was turned upside down. When I was twenty-three, it got flipped again. The same thing happened once more at twenty-four and the pattern continued so frequently, so frustratingly, that by the time I turned twenty-seven, I sincerely wondered if I would ever be able to say that I enjoyed being alive.

Life can really suck.

And while I'm no genius and I can't pretend to have the most traumatic story around, I truly do believe that everyone's story is valid. And everyone's pain is valuable *if* some useful lessons have been gleaned from the pain.

Let's just say that these past five years have been nothing but me relentlessly sowing into the field of faith, hoping that one day God would acknowledge my faithful efforts and bring forth some fruit. Little did I know that the desert years of my time on this earth were exactly what He wanted to *use* to cultivate and bring forth such fruit.

I am young.

I am a millennial.

And quite frankly, I make no apologies for my generation or my unique voice in this crowd. Because for every entitled brat who claims the term, there are just as many brilliant, kind, hard-working adults in the millennial category who hope to make a positive change.

And I am one of them.

You'll find that I'm full of contradictions. I'm a Christian but I still curse (please excuse my language in advance). I love God but sometimes I scream the very words that title this book, *"What the fuck, God?!"*

I am, and always have been, different.

By the time I reached the age of twenty-five, I was a bestselling author of five novels, owned a small press publishing company, and wrote, directed, hosted and produced a twenty-episode web series designed to equip people with tools to overcome depression.

Accomplishment.

Achievement.

That always gave me the biggest high.

And God must have known this. Because year after year after year, for every accomplishment He granted, He allowed life to hit me with failure blows, poverty punches, and heart-stabbing disappointments.

This book is for those of you who believed with all your heart that you would end up in one place and somehow, despite following God—or maybe even *because of it*—ended up on a completely different path.

This is for those of you who, though you love God, sometimes wonder who He even is.

And this is for those of you who, like me, cannot stand to see pain wasted.

Gleaning from the field of faith to build a richer, fuller, faith-filled life.

This book is for you.

-Michelle

CHAPTER ONE

Nothing is safe, everything's a risk

July 2013

"We're letting you go."

"What?"

I get surprised by a lot of things. The shitty thing about misfortune is there's never any warning when life deems it your turn to get screwed. But I didn't know the true, gut-wrenching depth of surprise until I heard those words.

"You're letting me go?" I repeated.

I've never been fired. I'm too young to be fired. People get fired when they have more to lose and at least a ten-year career under their belts. Or they get fired when they cop an attitude and pull some stupid shit at work. That's not me.

I'm twenty-two.

I just started. I was supposed to have seven weeks of training.

It's Monday of week four.

And I'm a good girl.

I've tried my hardest. I've never been late. I've commuted

two hours each way for this job, relieved that I would soon be moving—

Oh shit.

Oh shit!

"I'm supposed to be moving."

"What?" my former supervisor asks me. This small Asian lady with two toddlers and a soft-spoken voice regards me with eyes not malicious but firm in their delivery. I'm fired and there's not a damn thing I can say to get her to say otherwise; so I don't. They know I just signed a lease. They know I'm scheduled to move in on Thursday of this very week. We've only talked about it every day at lunch.

How am I going to get out of this?

My first apartment. In LA, of all places. There's no way I can afford it now.

It's not her problem.

She reaches behind her desk and gives me a light envelope. I peek inside as she says:

"Your final check, including eight hours today."

Damn.

I ask her why. She mutters some nondescript crap about how my attorney just "wasn't feeling it." Something about my needing specific directions and asking too many questions.

"I thought you told me to never assume anything," I remind her.

"You're in the legal field," she'd said. "Always be sure before you do something. Always double-check with your attorney."

I'd written it in all caps in my notes.

"John likes his legal assistants to be independent. He's very hands-off—"

As in lazy. What a jerk. I saw him only half an hour ago when he smiled and told me I was doing a good job. Went out of my way to get to know him. My birthday gift for him is sitting in my purse at my desk…well, former desk. I thought we were on the same page. I've never been so mistaken in my life.

I take the check, shake her hand, and walk out of her office. For some reason, she feels the need to accompany me down part of the hall. I assure her all of my things are in the same place and she lets me walk the rest of the way alone. Out of my peripheral vision, I see all of my office friends busy at work or joking around. I'm too shocked and embarrassed to tell them I won't see them tomorrow, and I haven't been here long enough to use the telltale box of collected office stuff. They're probably assuming I'm just leaving early, and I will neither confirm nor deny.

I'll probably cry at some point. Because the truth is, I feel like a colossal failure. This job was the only bright spot after getting rejected from all five grad schools I applied to months ago. A respectable, full-time job with the potential of benefits made my Facebooked life seem so much more promising. Now I'm back in the ranks of those "transitioning."

I make it home in just under two hours. It's a miracle I made it alive. I spent the entire ride illegally informing my inner circle of my recent unemployment. I reasoned that if I kept verbalizing, "I got fired," the reality of it would eventually sink in. The only thing better than a friend's sympathy is that of multiple friends.

As I walk into my rented room and kick off my $20 Comfort Plus heels, which won't be used tomorrow after all, I take stock of my situation. Twenty-four hours ago, I was a working woman with decent pay for someone fresh out of college in this economy. In two more months, my benefits would have kicked in. I remember feeling like I had passed some unspoken test of adulthood. That the real world started here: with a job and a place of my own; the means to support myself completely. I think I even wrote "#certifiedgrownup" on Twitter.

I shrug off my purse and lie on my bed. Remind myself that nothing else is happening immediately. That even though a major part of my world just imploded, I don't have to deal with any other blows this evening. I make a list. I have to deal with the apartment; wiggle out of that lease I just signed the day before. I'll probably get screwed out of the deposit, but I need to get my first month's rent back.

Next: the big picture issue. What the hell to do with my rotten excuse of a life? I've given my landlords notice. I have to leave in two weeks. I can't afford the studio in Van Nuys and jobs don't slide in quickly.

Go home, a little voice whispers inside.

And for once, in the three-and-a-half years I've been in California, I welcome it. Because the truth is, as I walked on the hot concrete of Milstein Adelman's parking lot, I felt almost as much relief as shock at the thought of being done.

4

Done with the two-hour commute.

Done with feeling like an idiot.

Done with studying the legal process and forgetting one stupid step.

Done with living in a city full of vapid, insincere people.

Done with being so far away from family.

From home.

I pick up the phone and make it brief before I change my stubborn mind again.

"Mom?" I pause. "I'm coming home."

• • •

That was five years ago.

When I graduated college, all I wanted was for things to click along and make sense and fall into the neat parameters of my master plan. I mean, I knew *He* had a master plan for me, but I thought my master plan fit perfectly in His master plan and that I was on my way to phenomenal success. But as you just read above, it simply didn't happen that way.

When an author starts a book, it is almost impossible to pick just the right beginning. I chose this moment for a reason. It was the start of real adulthood for me. Let's be honest; for most millennials, and maybe a generation or two before them, college is playacting adulthood. I was independent and learning, but still very much protected in the bubble of a small Christian university tucked in the suburbs of LA. The only real decisions I had to make were which classes I would take, how I would pay my way through school, and what I would do with my time. But for the most part, college leads you on a steady track.

I was spreading my wings—but not too much.

I recount this moment because it was my first real brush with adulthood and my first real taste of the setbacks, challenges, and decisions that would come to define my first five years post-college.

Nothing is truly safe.

That's what I learned in 2013. You can plan, you can strategize, you can do everything by the books…but in the end, *nothing* is a guarantee. There is no such thing as a "safe job," a "safe career path," a "safe life." I should have known this prior to getting fired.

My mom worked as an optometrist for over twenty years before suddenly losing her job during the 2008 recession. A single parent, she was the sole breadwinner of the family for as long as I could remember. And growing up, we lived a comfortable upper-middle-class lifestyle. I remember the abundance of my youth, when my mom made a robust salary and her income far exceeded her expenses. There was money for regular family vacations…trips to Disney World and Universal Studios. There was money for a time-share and annual vacations to Colonial Williamsburg. There was money for smaller things, like the full photo package from school pictures—and not just the basic portrait.

Then the recession hit.

The thing about poverty is that it tends to take root not only in your circumstances but also in your mindset. I would say even in your soul. When you stand in line at a food bank, have to apply for food stamps, and spend hours researching other government assistant programs…bit by bit you feel your dignity and abundance mindset begin to chip away. You become a survivor as opposed to a person purely enjoying the best that life has to offer. I didn't know how to view myself anymore. My family was poor.

Really poor.

Here's a *glimpse* of what we were to go through after my return to Maryland in 2013:

It started with the water heater. Over ten years old, the machine had begun leaking. Every day, my mom would go downstairs into the basement and try to sop up the liquid. Eventually, my sister and I were called in to help with the sopping-up shifts.

It just got worse.

The basement was slowly flooding. Mushrooms were appearing in the carpet. Despite our best efforts, we couldn't beat the insidious water. It eventually became so severe that we couldn't go down there anymore due to the mold developing.

And then…the tank stopped producing hot water.

From that day forward, we only had cold running water throughout the house. My mom had to tote buckets of boiling water to my grandmother so she could take a bath. As for me, I took advantage of my Planet Fitness membership and only took my showers at the gym.

In the midst of all this water chaos, we had a few unwelcome neighbors move in.

Not mice. But just as bad. Woodpeckers. A flock of bold birds pecked their way into our attic, set up nests, and started reproducing right in our house. The sound of pecking day in and day out, in what was normally a quiet home, was torturous, especially for me as a writer. We hired pest control to get rid of the first batch, but more came and we had no money to deal with it. I quickly realized that my writing sessions had to occur in the early mornings in order for me to keep my concentration intact. I began waking up at *2:30* in the morning to write before driving to the gym to work out and take a shower.

When we weren't concerned with these enormous issues, we were dealing with the never-ending problem of utility bills, repairs, and household expenses. Things that used to be so easy to take care of with the swipe of a card were now next to impossible to handle. I'll never forget having to confiscate wads of toilet paper because we'd run out and had no money to purchase new rolls.

I wasn't earning nearly enough to make a significant contribution and I felt guilty for in my own small way, adding to the financial burden my mom was already under.

When you experience poverty to that degree, you begin to wonder if this is a vortex you will ever escape.

Everything is a risk.

But could this vortex truly have been avoided? The truth is every decision you make comes with a risk. There are no safe bets. When I decided to go to Biola University, I assumed the risk of student loans. When I spent the first six months of my post-college life writing my debut novel while waiting for grad school decisions to come through, I took a risk. Granted, these were calculated risks in which I did my best to prepare for a favorable outcome.

I took out the loans with the full expectation that I would secure a profession that paid well enough for me to pay back my debts. I prepared well in advance of the six-month sabbatical I took and had more than enough saved and raised (through crowdfunding) to take the time to write *Type N*. I also believed I would get into at least one of the five schools I applied to; so I had a plan immediately following the book's release.

When my grad school plans failed, I jumped to Plan B: get a safe, full-time, entry-level job. Pay down some debts and reapply while working and supporting myself.

A reasonable plan.

So I went to the local temp agency and used two competing job offers to land the higher paying position of legal assistant. All smart moves. All thought out and prayed over. All very practical and full of common sense.

All blowing up in my face.

Everything is a risk. Nothing is safe. And I don't think it's meant to be—*especially* for a believer. Jesus didn't die on Calvary for us to live safe, risk-free lives. In Scripture, He repeatedly calls His people to do the inordinate, impractical, seemingly *stupid* because He desires to show His faithfulness in the most absurd settings.

If Moses could have picked the route out of Egypt, do

you honestly think he would have led a million people to the shores of the Red Sea? No one could have imagined the parting. No one. It had never been done before. Until then.

Recently, during my quiet time with the Lord, He had me reflect on this passage.

He asked me, "Michelle, what if the Israelites had decided to build rafts to try and escape the Egyptians? What if they chose to save themselves instead of throwing their full weight into My glory?"

"They would have died. Either drowned in the Sea or killed by the army behind them."

They did the foolish thing out of foolish trust. They took a risk and it paid off.

So what can we hold on to?

Faith.

Cue the inward groans.

I know. I get it. It is *such* a cliché.

But the annoying thing about clichés is that they are almost always the truth. God is referred to as The Rock over 1200 times in Scripture. He's repeatedly called The Rock of Israel, our fortress and protection, even our refuge. Think about the meaning of that symbol.

A rock.

The permanence, strength, and immovable nature of a rock is comforting against the ever-shifting landscape of life. When you cling to God, everything can fall to shit and you will still prevail. Nothing is safe. Everything's a risk. But

God is not. He doesn't change like shifting shadows (James 1:17). He doesn't change His mind (1 Samuel 15:29). He is literally the most stable being to ever exist.

Friend, if you feel like you're tossed and turned by life. If you wonder where you can go for safety, reassurance, comfort, sanity...look no further than Him.

When I lost my job in 2013, everything was topsy-turvy. Despite my initial call to my mother, I still debated about whether or not to leave California.

7/24/13

I was supposed to get my keys today. I would have been at MA a month today. I'm not as angry or despondent as I was earlier. Tim Keller has a way of smoothing out the rough edges. Now I just have a lot of questions. Will I get out of this apartment okay? Will I have any money to my name by the end of this? Should I stay in California or should I go home— back to Maryland?

My heart is torn. I'm nervous again that if I leave California, I will live to regret it. What am I gonna do in Maryland? I'm so confused.

Father, I don't know what You want from me. I have until the 15th—and then I gotta bounce. Big picture-wise, I don't know what You want. I formulated a plan in the parking lot of MA, but I don't know if You're in it or not.

What do you want? Tell me what you want?

I want to go to grad school. On the East Coast—

where I can see the leaves change color. I want my own place and a pet. Probably a dog. I want to move. Please talk to me, Lord. I thought this job was from You. I thought You wanted me to move closer to LA and really go for it. Why, Father? Why all this? Just as I'm about to take the leap—I get dropped like a hot potato. Why?

Why bring me so close to this new life only to have it go wrong? I'm out of a home in LA and I'm out of a home in La Mirada. What do You want from me?

Oh, dear. You feel so jostled about. I love you, Kirdledine. I have not abandoned you. I know the question burning in your mind.

Should I stay here, Lord?

No. You don't want to. You don't have to.

So I left.

CHAPTER TWO

Your feelings count

I love being a Christian.

It's challenging. It's fulfilling. It takes a ton of courage and a heart for risk that I never would have imagined prior to knowing God. It's maddening and frustrating and ridiculously confounding at times. But most importantly: it's the truth.

And at the end of the day, that's the only reason to ever follow anything. Is it the truth?

I believe Christ is.

So when I say anything that remotely criticizes Christianity or Christians—don't mistake me for a hipster millennial who's low-key apologizing for their faith. I'm not. I'm a believer and I will never be ashamed of Christ. Or my brothers and sisters in Christ. That said, I think it's healthy to question the status quo.

Like the Christian tendency to dismiss emotions as irrelevant. We've all heard it from various preachers and speakers.

"Faith over feelings."

"Live beyond your feelings."

"Elevate God's truth above your emotions."

At their core, these are all incredibly important tools to thrive in spite of life's circumstances. As someone who struggled with chronic clinical depression for ten years, I can personally attest to the importance of having a handle on your emotions. We've all had moments—days—when our emotions just took over and hijacked the driver's seat. But if that's your day-to-day experience (as it was once mine), things need to change so that your emotions aren't controlling you.

That said, I believe Christians have veered a little too far off course with regard to emotions. We're so guarded against our emotions taking precedence that we take it to the extreme and dismiss their relevance. This can be incredibly damaging to people who sense the world around them—and even God's Spirit within them—from an emotional perspective.

I would go so far as to wonder if the enemy targets people gifted with emotional sensitivity and twists this gift against them, using their heightened emotions to attack their mind, body, and relationships.

God's Guidance

Aside from the obvious effect of alienating believers who are more emotionally sensitive than others, sometimes the encouragement to shut our emotions off is tantamount to shutting off the voice of God in our lives. I firmly believe every believer has the capacity to hear the Lord and be guided by the Holy Spirit. When I became a Christian at seventeen, I quickly learned how I was able to hear Him. The "still small voice" so many speak of became a reality to me, and I began to home in on my ability to discern His voice from mine, the world's and the enemy's.

Other people discern His guidance by dreams. Or what they see in the Spirit. Some are guided exclusively through Scripture verses. I have family members who just know that they know in their "knower" when God is directing them to do something. It never ceases to amaze me how creative our God is. Why wouldn't He be just as creative in speaking to and guiding His children?

Over the years, I've discovered that while He has a primary way of speaking to me, He's not afraid to mix it up. Sometimes He'll repeat a verse or an idea to me through multiple people as a way to get my attention (this, by the way, is my favorite method of Him speaking to me). Other times, He'll have someone give me a prophetic word as they're praying for me. I've also gotten vivid dreams that I remember 80 percent of the time. I've had this gift since I was a child and a lot of times, God uses them as a way of communicating with me.

But other times…He simply uses my emotions. I once read an article in which a theologian claimed that our emotions are a gauge, not a guide. I beg to differ. I believe it is totally within God's prerogative to use our emotions however He chooses—as a gauge or a guide, at whatever time and under whatever circumstance He wants to.

He'll use our desires

In August 2013, I loaded all my earthly possessions into my '96 Nissan Maxima, set my GPS, and embarked on a cross-country trip: twenty-two years old, a woman, on my own. To this day, I look back at this five-day trip as one of the greatest adventures of my life. I still remember my grandmother's plea: "Michelle, I beg you—don't do it!"

All anyone could see was the danger associated with a young, attractive single woman traveling cross-country alone. I even joked about people finding my body in a ditch somewhere. (Don't ask me—I had a terrible sense of humor back then.) My dad urged me time and again to simply sell the car, ship my stuff, and fly back East. Looking back on it, though, I think I always wanted to do it. I wouldn't admit it to my parents or anyone else, but I'd always longed to do something wild and adventurous like travel cross-country alone while I was young—and this was the golden opportunity to do it.

Plus—I felt this assurance that I would be all right.

If I've learned anything about God in my millennial trek on this earth, it's that He's a pretty adventurous God. My family was shouting "No!" to me about this trip while His Spirit within me was shouting "Yes!"

At no point did God explicitly tell me to drive cross-country.

He certainly told me to leave California when I sought His guidance, but He didn't specify the *way* He wanted me to leave. In fact, it was fairly clear that the method was up to me. He just gave me a desire to drive and made it make sense to me financially.

Psalm 37:4 tells us that when we delight ourselves in the Lord, He will give us the desires of our hearts. Theologians have argued that this really means Christ will fashion our desires when we choose to put Him first in our lives. Meaning, if we have desires that don't align with His plans and purposes, He'll change them to better suit His plans, and our desires will perfectly match His as we revel in our relationship with Him.

I *love* that!

As a newborn Christian, I used to believe that following God meant torturing myself, saying no to all of the things that I wanted. I quickly learned, and experienced, that as I devoted myself and my affections to the God I loved, my heart began to change. My dreams shifted into something else altogether.

The first time I experienced this was in the summer before my freshman year of college. For all of my adolescence, I wanted to be an actress. And not just any actress. But an Academy Award-winning actress. I took acting lessons, participated in theater, even shot headshots with a talented classmate. But when the time came for me to attend New York University's prestigious Tisch School of the Arts, the Lord had changed my heart. I was no longer interested in performing other people's material. I became fascinated with the process of crafting the story as a filmmaker. I left NYU in the fall and transferred to Biola University's film school the following spring.

I never regretted it.

Christians often view the heart as wicked or deceitful because of Jeremiah 17:9. But the Word teaches that we are made new in Christ (2 Corinthians 5:17). With the Holy Spirit dwelling in me (1 Corinthians 3:16) and a new nature (Romans 6:6) taking dominion within me, I can trust that my heart is being steered by God; especially when I pray the prayer of surrender.

God, please mold my desires to perfectly match your own. If there is something I want that you don't want for me, please change my heart and remove that desire. Conversely, if there is something you desire for me that I don't yet want, please change my heart to want it. I want my desires to be perfectly aligned with yours and submitted to your will. In Jesus's Name.

Let's go back to August 2013. How miraculous is it for a completely loaded (possibly overloaded) seventeen-year-old vehicle to make a cross-country trek in the middle of the summer without a single breakdown? How miraculous is it that not once in all of the stops, motels, gas runs, and restroom breaks—not once did a vagrant touch the vehicle or attempt theft? I stopped at four motels in four different states without any issues, not to mention the numerous pit stops on the road.

God protected me *the entire journey*.

And I now have a beautiful experience that I can carry with me for the rest of my life.

Sometimes living a life of faith is acting on the desire God places within you and allowing Him to either course-correct you or confirm it by His grace.

In this case, He confirmed it and then some.

The warning system of God

I wish I could say the rest of 2013 was as glorious as a cross-country trek through the beauty of America.

It wasn't.

It was hard.

It was unpleasant.

I was miserable.

After all the fanfare died (my family still couldn't believe that I made that impossible trip), I was struck by three major realities: I was living with my mom again; I was broke as a joke; and I was feeling very, very unwell. Within a week of my arrival, I began to experience chronic nausea, numbing headaches, and a deep weakness and fatigue that wouldn't go away. No matter what I did—or what I took—I felt perpetually lightheaded and ill. It was as if the moment my body realized that I wasn't on the road, the minute I shot off the ignition in my mom's driveway, my body, too, checked out.

It ultimately took two months, three specialists and a new diet to pinpoint that the stress of the trip, combined with my poor eating habits on the road, took a serious toll on my body. Slowly but surely, I began to recover and shifted my focus to making the most of this new season.

And that was a mission in and of itself.

What do you do when you end up in a place you never thought you'd be in?

I was struggling with my new lot in life. Going from being a thriving young adult, independent and making my own money, to living in my childhood room bruised my ego even more than losing my job did. I felt like a loser. Despite my illness, I immediately set out to look for work and discovered the cold Southern Maryland truth: jobs were not that plentiful in or around Waldorf, Maryland. I was a new graduate with minimal experience still in the midst of the financial recession. And with a film degree, emphasis in screenwriting, I had little to offer to the already sparse economy.

I got a part-time job at Family Christian, selling Christian goods and struggling to keep a good attitude. Not only were we paid minimum wage, the business wasn't doing too well and we had more employees than we needed— making hours minimal and pay unreliable.

Immediately, I sought the Lord for counsel. And as always, He responded in turn…

> *You just do as I say. Persevere at Family Christian, lay your boundaries, do your best and save where you can. …Michelle, what bothers you the most is not a lack of moving forward. You __are__ moving forward. You just don't feel it. And things aren't clicking along as fast or as cohesively as you like. My Child, sometimes it takes just as much courage to wait as it does to take a risk… It's true, you are working a job that's beneath you, that you are overqualified for. But it is temporary and there is good that will come from it. Just do the best you can and I will continue to bless your hands.*
>
> *What can I be doing better?*

You can wait better.

Slowly but surely, I found myself focusing on the aspects of my job that were fulfilling. I began to view Family Christian as my current place of ministry. Who was I ministering to? My customers. I helped each person with gusto. I served them with a selfless attitude. And I stopped and prayed with several people who made it very clear that they were hurting and needed God.

I put the well-known phenomenon to the test and discovered it was true: every time I took my eyes off myself, even for just a four-hour shift, I was able to pour into someone else and feel a deep sense of fulfillment. I wasn't where I wanted to be by a long shot, but I knew I made a difference in someone's life in that moment.

Because of my exemplary service, I excelled in that tiny shop.

But what do you do when you face what looks like a total dead end?

Despite the moment-to-moment joy I could derive from helping others at Family Christian, I was *still* desperate for a new direction. It was around this time, in my endless search for a way out of this season, that I stumbled upon a new company called Upstart. Upstart, at the time, was an income-sharing platform that distributed money to qualified applicants who in turn pledged a certain percentage of their income for a predetermined number of years. It was an interesting, new, mostly untested concept, and I dove headfirst into the application. I wanted to use those funds to build my fledgling publishing company (MNO Media), write and self-publish more books, and apply to a variety of prestigious creative writing MFA programs.

My proposal worked, I was accepted, and was soon offered $12,000.

I was excited. I was scared. I was hopeful. I was really scared.

And ultimately it came down to making my biggest financial decision since choosing to accept student loans for my education. I prayed. And for the first time in my Christian walk, I felt a deluge of confusion clouding my ability to hear God's voice crystal clearly. Looking back on it, I believe the enemy was attempting to disguise himself as Light and mimic the voice of God. So, in quick procession, the following occurred:

I "heard" God (really the enemy) saying "Yes."

I accepted.

I *immediately* felt zero peace.

I recanted my acceptance.

The peace came flooding back.

And I never regretted withdrawing my acceptance.

In the end, despite their numerous attempts to convince me they were not a lending entity, Upstart did end up becoming a personal lending company. I'm not 100% certain, but there is a good chance that my income share experience would have turned into a $12,000 loan had I accepted the money.

So alongside learning about God's will through my *desires*, He taught me about *feeling* His answer versus only *hearing* His answer. We're human. And it is human nature to hear our voice as God's voice when we really want a specific outcome. I felt that lack of peace as God's internal red flag.

I'd never made a decision before where I felt like throwing up afterward.

The swift removal of peace was so powerful, so overwhelming, I could not for the life of me ignore it or brush it off as nerves. It was as if the hand of God touched my chest and would not let my heart palpitate normally *until* I rectified my mistake.

A sense of dread and uneasiness filled my gut and wouldn't abate until I withdrew my acceptance.

I thank God that He used such a visceral response to course-correct me.

In the end, I created a crowdfunding campaign to start MNO Media debt-free. It worked and I raised just enough capital to get my start.

I often think of that period of my life; that moment when I felt my Spirit warn me almost violently. What I didn't know at the time was that this experience was just the beginning of training me to follow His lead above all others—myself included.

CHAPTER THREE

Presumption is not the same as faith

Columbia.

Anyone who knows me can easily tell you how important that single name is to me, my walk with the Lord, and my understanding of God.

At the end of 2013, I was busy working on my second novel, a romance, called *Remember Me*. I managed to apply to several grad schools by the skin of my financial teeth. And I also managed to work and save just enough money to quit my little part-time job and focus on writing until I—hopefully—received admission into one of the universities I applied for. Looking back on it, in a way, I was doing the exact same thing that I had done the previous year.

Only this time, I was two books in, I applied to more schools, and I diversified the programs that I was applying to. For some reason, I couldn't get past the feeling that I did not make the most of my film school education at Biola University. I knew the fundamental ideological principles of evangelical Christianity inside and out—or so I thought. I knew what I believed about God.

The unique thing about Biola University is that every student who graduates, graduates with a minor in theological studies because thirty units of Bible courses are grafted into our curriculum.

So A+ on the Bible education.

But my path as a film student at Biola was a very unique, difficult, and harrowing experience. With a seven-to-three male-to-female ratio, I never felt fully confident or comfortable being a female film student. The technical courses were complicated from day one and I never truly mastered the production, cinematography, or audio components of my film education. Although I took courses in all of these areas, I still felt extremely deficient in the field. Part of it was Biola University's fault, but most of it was mine.

I should not have allowed myself to be intimidated by the ridiculous number of men in the program. I should have bitten the bullet and purchased my own film equipment with my meager student earnings. This would have allowed me the chance to experiment. The opportunity to learn on my own time and at my own pace all that I needed to know about the technical aspects of creating a film—and to do so without the risk of damaging the school's equipment. I allowed myself to get psyched out and as a result, I failed to make the most of what could have been a decent film education.

I think what really got to me was that I graduated with a degree in film, but the only area of film that I felt confident in was my emphasis: screenwriting. This meant that when I entered the workforce, I could not in all decency apply for videography positions or media posts. How could I apply to be the editor of a church's media team when I barely knew how to operate Final Cut Pro?

I felt angry—at the school, at my experience, but especially at myself for being so ill-equipped in the one thing that I earned my degree in. So I decided to get my master's and to diversify my application pool by applying to both creative writing programs and film schools! I researched a plethora of film schools, but the only one that made my heart leap was Columbia University. It was an Ivy League school, their coursework and teaching philosophy appealed to me, and it was based in New York City, giving me yet another state with which to embark on a fresh start.

As 2014 came around, I felt as if things were finally starting to change for the better. I'd left my job, I was writing full-time, I'd just learned that I was accepted for an all-expenses-paid writing retreat in Martha's Vineyard that spring, and I felt very optimistic about my chances of getting into Columbia—especially after they contacted me for an interview. I was also getting stronger physically. I had established a workout routine and was feeling fully recovered from the illness that took me by surprise the previous year. A Christian summer camp hired me to serve as a camp counselor in Maine. I was set to enjoy adventures left and right before starting the next phase of my academic career.

Or so I thought.

In April, I heard from Columbia again. I received a letter

from them informing me that I had been wait-listed for their program.

For some reason, it never occurred to me to consider being wait-listed as a possible outcome. I tended to view things in black and white—either they want you or they don't. This in-between space felt like an unexpected and unwanted academic purgatory. Really, it was a purgatory on my future. Placing me on hold until they saw fit to give me their final answer. By this time, the other universities had said no. All my bets were on this prestigious school that took the time to interview me and didn't seem quite ready to let me go.

I still remember my initial response to that letter. And to be honest, I wish I'd reacted in a different way. Because the minute I finished reading their notification, I went straight to my mom's room and told her the news. My mom, in turn, instructed me to start claiming my place and my position as a Columbia student, regardless of what that letter said.

Hence, the title of this chapter.

The Columbia Way

I ended up learning in a really painful yearlong journey that presumption is not the same as faith. For the remainder of that spring and all of that summer, I continued to tell myself, and others, that I was going to Columbia University. I said it as if it was a fact and I declared the "truth" to myself every single morning.

I even created a declaration sheet that I recited to myself

every single day. I printed a copy of it, and framed it, before posting it on my wall, right next to the waitlist letter above my desk. And next to that declaration sheet? An empty frame, waiting to be filled with a final acceptance letter from Columbia.

So much happened in 2014.

I published my second novel and it became a bestseller. I went to that writing retreat in Martha's Vineyard, and it was a time that changed my life as I communed with God and learned of His plans for my life. I served at a Christian camp as a counselor in an experience that ultimately redeemed a previously traumatic one. But for some reason, in my insistence that Columbia *had* to be my next step, my bright hope, my good fortune—2014, to me, was all about Columbia University.

I felt so certain that because I was following the formula of prayer, tithing, and most importantly, declaration, I *had* to be accepted into their film program. It never occurred to me to stop and realize that I was trying to dictate to the God of the universe what my future needed to be. I fell headlong into the name-it-and-claim-it trap. A trap that my mother unintentionally guided me to.

And it wasn't her fault. It was mine.

Because after receiving a world-class theological education from one of the leading Bible colleges in the country, I *knew better* than to fall for that trap! The truth was, I made Colombia such an idol (because of every hope and dream I had attached to getting in) that I willfully believed it was my destiny to go to the school.

What to believe

Declarations are a beautiful thing. Faith is a beautiful and oh so necessary part of life. But there is a huge difference between having faith for something God *says He will do* and presuming to believe that your faith will make something happen, even if it is *not* God's will. The truth is, I should have stopped the minute I received that waitlist letter and asked my Heavenly Father if Columbia was His plan for me. I was in prayer the entire time that I researched, applied, and interviewed with the school. And I don't believe I was outside of His will in going through the process. But when I received that letter, I failed to go to Him first. In my heightened emotion, I went straight to my mother and jumped on the name it-claim-it train to get my way.

I took that strategy so far that I misled people to believe that I actually had an acceptance letter from Columbia University. I reasoned to myself that I was not lying, but that I was calling those things that were not as though they were in faith (Romans 4:17). But God will not back up something that is not in His will.

I see now how arrogant I was in that entire process. Because the Lord Himself was trying to communicate to me that I wasn't going to get in.

Yes, my friend! You heard me right.

He gave me several dreams in which I received their final decision, and every single time: it was a firm "No"!

What did I do in my name-it-and-claim-it frenzy?

I rebuked the dream!

I declared even harder that things would work out the way *I* wanted them to, and I refused to believe for even a moment that God would not answer this prayer.

Talk about night and day from Biola.

A healthier way.

I've been wait-listed once in my life before.

When I was a freshman at New York University (circa 2009), I took a huge leap of faith and, believing this was God-led, withdrew from the university to attend Biola University. The only problem was, while I had received acceptance into the university at large, there was a separate application process for their film school. Since it was highly competitive, there was a very real possibility that I might not be accepted into their program. But I took the risk and transferred, traveling across the country, away from family, all to pursue a program that I hadn't been accepted into yet. I believed God was calling me to study there and that He would open the right doors for me.

I transferred in the spring, and the entire semester revolved around whether or not I would get into the only program I felt I was called to go to Biola for. In the end, surprise, surprise: I got wait-listed. I'd never been wait-listed in my life, and I had no idea what to do with that. After asking numerous film students and even the department secretaries about what being wait-listed meant, I ultimately had to come to terms with the fact that I would either be accepted or I wouldn't.

There wasn't much I could do to alter the situation… except pray.

So that's what I did.

I got everyone in my circle to pray for me. Friends, family, professors. But I took it a step further and began waking up every morning at five a.m. to go to our school's track and walk it while petitioning the Lord in prayer for my spot in the program. I reminded God of how far He brought me, of the huge risk I took in leaving a well-known university to attend a little-known Christian college. I asked the Lord to honor my faithfulness and my willingness to risk it all, by opening the spot for me.

I will never forget when, one day, towards the end of my ceaseless prayers, the Lord suddenly interrupted me and said, "Shut up, Michelle."

I paused.

"Did you just tell me to shut up?"

Yes, He did.

He told me, "Michelle, what do you think I have been doing this entire time you have been petitioning me to get into the film program?"

And as if He cued a short film to play in my mind, He quickly showed me all of the events and conversations and opportunities I'd had in recent weeks to experience the film program. I'd gone to showings, info nights, and happened to meet a plethora of students *and professors* already in the program to get a taste of what it was I was petitioning for.

He then told me, "Michelle, I'm trying to get you excited about what I'm about to give you."

Two days later, I received my acceptance letter.

What did I do right in this situation? When I got the waitlist notification, I didn't assume anything. I asked for prayer and was honest about my standing with the program. I admitted to others and myself that there was a real possibility I might not get in. And I petitioned the Lord with open hands to please open that door for me if indeed it was His will for me to be there. In the end, He confirmed it right before I got in by giving me showings, connections, and a variety of experiences to whet my appetite for what He was about to usher me into.

And on top of that, in His grace, He flat-out told me, "This is what I have for you. This is what I've been doing. My answer is yes."

And then—He did it.

As I look back on that experience compared to Columbia, the humility of my heart stands out to me. I wasn't assuming anything about the situation. I was honest in what I wanted but fully acknowledged that it might not be what He wanted. My faith was ultimately in *Him* and *His* hands as opposed to *my desires* and *my manipulation*. I often wonder what would have happened if I had simply used the template of my Biola experience for my Columbia one?

But a story without conflict isn't really a story, is it?

Don't Columbia yourself

Learn from my mistake, friend. Be careful to not assume or presume God's will for your life. Or even the *way* that He wants to bring about His will for your life. It is extremely important to have faith in God, and what He says, and even, to a degree, in yourself. But choose to do this from His truth and His word as opposed to your idols.

It will save you so much grief.

CHAPTER FOUR

Saying yes to God often feels like saying no to common sense

WTF, God!

Seriously.

What was I going to do now?

I still remember sitting in my bedroom wondering how the hell I ended up that situation. There sat my suitcase in the middle of my bedroom and—in faith!—I packed it with just enough stuff to tide me over for my first few nights in New York City. I hadn't received the final notification from Columbia, and I still believed that I was going to get in.

I declared it, I confessed it, I believed with all my heart that it was going to happen. I believed so hard that I even turned in my Maryland license plates for my car. I reasoned to myself, *I'll be living in New York. I'm not going to need this vehicle.* I did every single action I could think to do to express my faith and communicate to the Lord that I was ready for this next step in my life.

But it didn't happen.

On the first day of school, when classes officially began at

Columbia, I still had not heard back from the university. In the end, I got a letter from the school *four days* after the start of classes, informing me of what I already knew deep inside.

It wasn't going to happen.

I wasn't going to grad school.

To say that I was in a tailspin would be the understatement of the decade. I had no idea what the hell I was going to do. I didn't know if I should attempt to apply for grad school again or just call uncle. I didn't know what type of career to pursue or how to get to where I wanted to be in my life.

In fact, I was seriously questioning what I actually wanted out of life after all.

Where do you go from where I was? What do you do when the doors keep slamming shut in your face, you have real bills to pay, and you need to find direction to keep from losing your shit? I simply didn't know what to do. I emailed old professors, asking for advice. I inquired left and right about what it was that I needed to do. Finally, I made myself be still and approach the one Person I felt most betrayed by: the Lord.

I prayed.

I woke up early in the morning, as was my custom, and I let the Lord have it. All of my frustration. All of my anger. The feeling of betrayal was palpable. I remember telling my mother and friends that I felt like I was on a raft in the middle of the ocean with no land to paddle to. All I could see was water everywhere, with no markers, no direction, no guidance.

And I was very honest with the Lord about this.

Laying it all out

If there's one guiding principle I have always used in my relationship with the Lord, it's that honesty truly is the best policy. Growing up, I used to believe there were limits to what you could and could not say to God. He is, after all, the creator of the universe and if He wanted to, He could smite me with His very breath. Even as a small child, I always believed in having a reverential respect for His holiness, His justice, His righteousness, and His omnipotence.

It took really coming to know Him my junior and senior year of high school to realize that the only way to have an authentic relationship with Him was to keep it 100. And as I progressed to college, and the various trials *that* presented, I engaged in truly visceral fights with the Lord.

Not necessarily Jacob versus Angel of the Lord type fighting (Genesis 32:22-32). But more along the lines of a screaming toddler punching and kicking her ever-so-patient Father. This level of honesty progressed to such a degree that I actually became comfortable with the idea of cussing God out. A pastor at my church preached that God could take anything you throw at Him, including outright rage. And me being me, I tested this for myself.

I was around twenty years old. I had so much rage inside of me because of all the drama I was going through that any little thing would set me off. If a driver cut me off, I would lean on my horn, New York-style. If a student was passive-aggressive with me, I called them out on their shit. I had no regard for other people's feelings and I became an expert at using my writing ability to cut people down with my razor-sharp words. I had zero patience for fools, time-wasters, and anyone who stood in the way of what I wanted; and I would lash out—almost exclusively at God.

Friend, can I tell you? God can take your shit. He can take your anger. He can take your lashing. He can take your irrational rage. *He can take it all.* Like any normal relationship, you have to deal with conflict. It is the only way to test your love. You will never have a truly intimate relationship with the Lord until you feel comfortable enough to reveal *all* of your heart to Him: the good, the bad, and the downright nasty.

I'm not saying you should have knockdown, drag-out fights with Him on a regular basis. But everyone needs to experience it once to know that God is a safe friend, a true confidante, the Only One who can fully handle all of you, flaws and all.

I'll never forget when I was visiting a friend and I couldn't find her apartment. This was during my twenty-year-old, raging angry chick phase. I didn't know where to park, my GPS was acting crazy, it was night, and I was already late—a recipe for total disaster. I finally found a parking space, and then I realized that the gift I brought my friend as a "thank you for hosting me" had slipped into some godforsaken crevice in my car.

As I searched, trying to squeeze my hand in one tiny space after another, the rage boiled up in me, like the water in a kettle. Finally, I lost my cool, and I exploded at the Lord. As I sat in my little '96 Nissan Maxima, windows rolled up and sealed, I screamed at Him about my frustration.

Why couldn't He make things easier for me? Why did everything have to be so damn difficult? Why was everything going wrong when I was *already* late?

But I held back the one thing that I really, really felt at the core of my being. It was screaming in my heart, but years of religious conditioning told me I could never say it aloud. And this was where the Lord nudged me. He nudged me.

He told me in the Spirit, "Say what you need to say. Go ahead, say it."

I couldn't hold it back anymore.

I screamed aloud, "FUCK YOU!"

I have no words for the rush of relief I felt after screaming those words. It was as if everything pent up in me finally had an outlet, and I was coming face-to-face with the truth of how I felt. Who was I, a mere mortal of flesh and bones, to speak that way to my Lord and Savior? And why on earth would He actually *invite me* to do it?

It was simply His kindness.

And His grace.

And you know what He said in response?

"I'm here. I love you. And that isn't going to change."

My anger vanished. I found my friend's home and I had a wonderful night with dear sisters. God didn't blow me up. He didn't lash out in return. He kindly accepted my repentance when I was in my right mind, and He assured me that my standing with Him would have remained the same whether I tried to make amends or not.

He knew it needed to come out of me, regardless of how ugly it really was. He knew that having the emotions roll inside of me would do nothing but turn me into a bitter woman. The same way the pus in an infected wound must come out in order to heal, the darkest truths of our hearts and minds must be released directly to the Lord to make way for His healing power.

I carried this memory with me into the conversation about Colombia. I wasn't enraged and emotionally out of control like I was at twenty, but I *was* deeply hurt and severely disappointed.

The "insanity" of God

I was at a crossroads.

I either had to find a job or use the last of my savings to a.) apply for grad school again and b.) attempt to release two more books that the Lord placed on my heart to write. By this time, I had numerous letters, requesting I follow up my debut novel, *Type N*, with a sequel. Because my royalty checks were still pretty handsome from the romance novel I released earlier that year, it was easy for me to start work on the sequel, *Taking Names*.

I also felt the Lord giving me the release to apply for grad school one more time.

Once again, I applied to Columbia University, with the hope that maybe I would receive a more favorable outcome the second time around. I applied to a few other film programs as well, but I was really gunning for Columbia. As far as I was concerned, it was either now or never.

Literally.

Because this was my third time applying for grad school, I promised myself that this would be the last time I would submit an application. There is something about subjecting yourself to an endless purgatory of sorts. For more than two years, my life had been on hold as I waited month after month for university after university to inform me of their decisions. The waitlist process exacerbated this by an additional six months.

I was doing stuff in the meantime, yes. I was actually accomplishing things that people my age didn't typically accomplish.

But I still felt like I was spinning my wheels.

I wanted to move on *to* my life as well as *with* it. And for two years, I thought grad school was going to *be* that life. For the first time since graduating Biola, I had to come to terms with the fact that it might not be in the cards for me. This was doubly confusing considering the fact that I *asked* the Lord time and again if this was where He wanted me to go next.

Where the hell was His direction in this?

There comes a point in life when you have to decide to nip the bud. An author friend of mine counseled me, "Michelle, there have been so many times that I have forced a door to open that God wanted to remain shut. If you push hard enough and long enough, it will open and you will end up on a detour you never needed to be on."

That was all the warning I needed.

I pledged to myself that if the third time wasn't the charm, it would be the last time I put myself in this purgatory. I asked the Lord to reveal His will in a really practical way: either close the door once and for all via rejections, or open the door at last as an indication that this really was His will for me. I wanted to move on, one way or the other. And it helped to remind myself of the definition of insanity: doing the same thing over and over again and expecting a different result.

It was one thing to try to get into grad school for a year or two, but to put my life on perpetual hold, making my decisions based on whether or not a committee decided to choose me, was not the type of life I wanted to lead. I wasn't going to waste my youth.

So during the fall of 2014, I sent in applications and I worked on my third novel. It was at this point that I came into my own as an author. I finally mastered my writing technique, the schedule, and the method that I needed to implement in order to finish a book by a specific deadline. In three weeks, I finished the book and I released it to a small readership who took the title to Amazon Kindle's bestsellers list in the science fiction category.

Great, right? I had three bestsellers on my roster. I was going for grad school one more time. And who knew? Maybe things would turn around at last.

But they didn't.

While *Taking Names* briefly hit the bestsellers list for science fiction, it never generated the sort of income that *Remember Me* did. Science fiction money was not the same as romance money. The truth was, I now had established two different readerships: readers who loved me for my romance writing and readers who loved my science fiction work.

That doesn't make for financially prosperous writing.

To top it off, the royalties from *Remember Me* were really starting to dwindle down. It was the end of the year and I was reaching a pretty critical point in my finances. Leading up to the holidays, I had just enough money to either get another job so I could keep paying my bills or take a risk and continue writing, banking on this project being a success.

Once again, I went on a walk and prayed to the Lord about what it was He wanted me to do. I've always had the mindset that it is better to seek His face and His will directly as opposed to guessing my way into a future He never wanted for me. To my surprise, the Lord made it very clear what He wanted me to do in this instance.

"Write the book," He said. "I will bless it immensely and it will be a blessing to those who read it."

Now I had another choice to make.

Obey or ignore.

Checking your brain at the door

There will be times in this life when God doesn't make a stitch of sense.

In fact, I think He likes to do this more often than not. I think He says to Himself, *let me come up with the craziest, most creative, most nonsensical method and test my child's faith by asking them to do what simply doesn't make sense to them.*

He did it with the Israelites at the Red Sea (Exodus 14).

He did it with Joshua at the walls of Jericho (Joshua 6).

He did it with Gideon and his 300 men (Judges 7).

God's ways are sometimes utterly ridiculous, simply because He must get the credit. I really should have titled this chapter, "When Saying Yes to God Feels Like Chucking Your Brain." It goes against the grain of what your common sense tells you to do. And it always involves a risk.

Can I encourage you to simply say yes to Him? I know it's scary when He calls you to do something that you never would have thought to do. I was scared shitless when I made the decision to go full speed ahead with *Jane,* my fourth novel.

I knew it was a decision that would make or break me.

CHAPTER FIVE

God is faithful

God is faithful.

That should go without saying, shouldn't it? But let's be honest here. Every Christian has a moment, or multiple moments, or endless moments, of wondering if God really is faithful. If He really will do what He says He'll do.

And I've come to learn that the only way to know for yourself is by going through His faith test...or tests.

As I turned twenty-four years old that January, it occurred to me that I really was at the edge of my sanity. I'd gone through so much since graduating from Biola and I was frustrated that, despite earning my bachelor's degree, despite my best efforts, I was still a grown woman living at home with her mom, trying to figure it out—and not really knowing what the end goal was.

I could go into detail about the writing process, but no one really wants to hear that.

Suffice it to say, at the end of 2014, the Lord gave me February 7th as the release date for my fourth novel, *Jane*. I balked at how quickly that date was approaching. When I did the math, I realized that I was giving myself just five weeks to write the longest novel I had written yet.

But because of my work on *Taking Names*, I had my writing process down to a science. I knew—and did—exactly what needed to be done to reach my target deadline. And by some miracle, I finished writing the draft for the 130,000-word novel in just five weeks.

As the writing progressed, Christmas came and went. New Year's passed. My birthday even flew by. Nothing was going to get my mind off of my goal of completing this book in time. All my eggs were in this basket. If the book succeeded, it would be well worth the risk. But if it failed, I was up the creek without a paddle. Gone were my days of total risk aversion.

Oddly enough, it was around this time that the Lord decided to punctuate my faith journey with an even more serious test of faith.

Insert wisdom teeth testimony.

Losing my teeth, gaining more wisdom

Four years prior, around the time I was twenty, I began to notice my wisdom teeth emerging. Initially an irritation, by the time I graduated college, they really started hurting me. Despite medicating it, the pain became persistent and I became concerned.

In 2008, my pediatric dentist had warned me as a young—and stupid—teen that they would be impacted and I should probably have them removed, but he didn't stress the issue and I—stupidly—decided not to have them extracted.

Little did I know that my mom would lose her job soon after, we wouldn't have insurance, and my insurance in college would not cover the cost of dental exams, let alone surgical extractions. So for four years, I endured the teeth in pain, hearing at every cleaning I managed to pay for out of pocket that the four teeth needed to be extracted sooner rather than later. One dentist—who was more like a miserly mechanic than a dentist—offered me a "deal" of $200 per tooth. I later learned that it *was* a deal because I then heard quotes ranging from $300 to $600 *per* tooth in 2014.

By the end of the year, the pain and inconvenience of it all, plus the fear of getting an infection in one particular tooth, got so bad that I started frantically searching for affordable options.

None were coming up.

In the early mornings, I worked on *Jane* but during the rest of the day, I kept searching for a way to remove the teeth. Between my regular bills, the production cost of *Jane,* and other financial obligations swiftly approaching (including a friend's wedding), I knew that I needed a miraculous way to get all four teeth out within my tiny budget.

Finally, I prayed.

And I asked others to pray.

I literally wrote on my morning prayer list under "Pressing/Short-Term Needs": "Wisdom teeth removal— NIH or some other free/reduced means." I prayed hardcore for at least two or three months.

Finally, a breakthrough came.

Someone told me of a clinic at the University of

Maryland in Baltimore that did oral surgery for a reduced price in their School of Dentistry in order to train their students under careful medical supervision. The price quoted to me by them was anywhere from $126 to $380 per tooth. I thought, *Okay, go for it. At least get this ONE particular tooth out.*

I had to wait until the next year, late January, to be seen, and I went with the hope and prayer that I would return without this one particular tooth in my mouth.

I didn't.

"I'm so sorry, but your case is more complicated and requires a licensed dentist."

When I arrived, got examined, and had my case reviewed, the dental students told me that contrary to what they originally thought, the angle of my impaction would make my extraction far more complicated than what they were qualified to handle as students. I would have to get not one, but two teeth removed at minimum, raising the cost. Not only would I have to come back for a first-year resident to do it, but I would also have to pay triple the price they quoted me, more than $600, to get it done.

Spiraling out

I was horrified, bitterly disappointed, and so, *so* hurt. It took everything for me to scrounge the gas money, X-rays, and minimum funds for the procedure.

"Please," I begged the student. He looked at me, his eyes kind. "I barely had the gas money to make the trip out here.

I am in so much pain and really need this tooth out. Even if it's just this *one* and I have to pay more, can you please do this extraction?"

They still said no.

I had to come back.

And that, ladies and gentlemen, was where I really lost my shit.

I broke down. I literally cried in the clinic.

The student felt moved enough to do some research for me and informed me of a grant that the university had for reducing the cost of procedures on a need basis. But I would still have to come back to get the whole thing done. In my mind, the trip was a waste.

Do you know that feeling you get when you have to use the restroom and the closer you get to it, the more pressing your need is to go? It felt that way with my mouth. By the time we got to the clinic, it was pounding in pain.

Only for us (my mom drove me) to leave without any work being done.

Extremely upset, I left the clinic and cried all the way home. I kept asking God why and the only answer I got was, "I want a more qualified person to do the job." So I resolved to wait.

Drained, I filled out the application, scanned and emailed it to the contact person and prayed, wondering why a day full of promise became a complete nightmare and waste of time. We'd spent five hours there only for me to go home with all four teeth still in my mouth.

Miracles

God is not a man that He should lie.

The next morning, I received a call from the clinic. The contact person I sent my application to heard of my experience and apologized for what went down. She told me that my application for the grant had been approved and offered to have all four of my wisdom teeth—*all four of my wisdom teeth*—removed for just over $200!

Reeling in shock, I vaguely heard her add, "I want to help you get those teeth out as soon as possible since I know you're in pain. I can get you in here earlier. How's this Friday for you?"

I was scheduled for the next Tuesday. Had I waited for that day, I would not have seen anyone because we ended up having a blizzard that shut down most roads and closed the clinic.

Friend: God knew *exactly* when I needed to be seen and *exactly* what would delay me if I waited any longer. I came in that Friday, got all four teeth removed by a licensed doctor, not a student, and only spent roughly $60 per tooth as opposed to the $600 quoted to me.

In my short-sighted haste, I nearly missed out on the best God had for me. I went from begging to pay more to only get half the job done by a student, only to have God provide for the full need at less than half the price by someone who was more qualified.

GOD. IS. FAITHFUL. #justsayin

This happened at the end of January. I was smack dab in the middle of editing *Jane* and the release date was quickly approaching. I had numerous readers reaching out to me, letting me know how excited they were about the book's upcoming release. I had already given previews of the story and a peek at the cover. Come hell or high water, this book was going to be released and it had to be released on February 7th.

By some miracle, even as I was tending to my surgical wounds and trying to avoid dry socket, I stayed on schedule with the production of the book. On February 7th, *Jane* was released. And I began a month-long marketing blitz to draw attention to the novel and make it as financially successful as it could be within my limited budget.

God had already shown me how faithful He was the previous month.

In providing for my surgery, He'd taken care of an issue that had plagued me for years on end, and He did it in such a way that I would never have to worry about that same issue again. I went into the release of *Jane* knowing that God was faithful.

But little did I know that His faithfulness can sometimes blow you out of the water.

Jane quickly became an international bestseller. The novel remained on a variety of Amazon bestsellers lists for more than two months straight. My first major check for the book was around $5,000.

For someone who had a total of $300 left to her name, this was gargantuan.

I never knew that my writing could earn me so much.

I invested about $500 to produce *Jane*.

I received ten times the investment back on the first month's royalty alone.

The book went on to gross several thousand more dollars and ended up sustaining me for the remainder of the year. It has sold better than all of my previous books combined. And I still receive royalty checks from the Kindle and print versions, alongside the audio version that we recently released.

But even greater than the financial reward of this novel was the readers' response to it.

After a few initial reviews from beta readers and friends, *Jane* took on a life of its own in the market. Women from all stages of life, in numerous countries, reached out to me in a slew of letters and notes, thanking me for writing the story. In the book, the main character has suffered from a variety of abuses and must overcome her internal wounds in order to embrace real love with another; as well as discover the truth of God's character. you

I received letters from women sharing their survival stories. I received letters from women who struggled with their faith in God and needed this book to reconcile themselves to Him once and for all. I received letters from mothers who bought the book for their daughters. I received letters from both believers and non-believers who credit the story as part of their healing journey.

In the end, the Lord perfectly answered the prayer that I prayed at the very outset of this project: that this book would bless me financially and bless others spiritually. To this day, I still receive letters from women, thanking me for writing *Jane*.

I look back on 2015 as the true anchor point in my life. I took a risk and said yes to God, ultimately saying no to my brain and my common sense, to obey Him and do what I felt He was calling me to do. This particular situation in my life ingrained a lesson that I believe God wanted to sear into my core. And I believe that He wants to sear it into yours.

Friend, God is faithful.

It is easy as believers to proclaim that He is good. That despite whatever is going on in the world, and our lives, He is good and He makes all things work together for our good (Romans 8:28). But understanding and receiving His faithfulness is a completely different story.

It is the difference between believing that God *can* do something and knowing He will. It's the difference between knowing that God is loving and feeling He actually loves you. It is the difference between knowing that God can take care of you and being confident that He will. It is the difference between being a casual observer of the God of Israel, and experiencing Him up close and personal as Jacob did (Genesis 32:22-32).

Throughout my Christian walk, I've sought stability from a multitude of sources: money, significance, education, career strategizing. It's as if it took God all of my college years and, so far, all of my post-college years, to drive home the point that He is the only firm foundation. He's the only one you can truly count on. And while life's circumstances try to lie and say otherwise, the truth is, He will always come through in the end.

As a faithful God, He has no other choice.

God's faithfulness is who He is, not what He chooses.

Whatever you're going through in your life, at this moment, never forget to tell yourself that God is faithful. It is His faithfulness that holds you secure.

CHAPTER SIX

There is always more

There is always more. I can't put my finger on when it started, but it was sometime during college. Even though I was learning so much about the Lord and theology, I felt this hunger and this thirst to know more of God.

I didn't know how to make my faith work.

I didn't know why, even though I believed in Christ, even though Scripture said I was a new creation, I still struggled with sin. I struggled with rage, judging others, and lust. Addictions that had formed as a teenager still remained.

I'll just lay it all out here right now.

When I was a child, I was molested by a family friend. And by the time I reached adulthood, I was full-blown addicted to pornography. You don't hear too many women talking about this issue. It is widely considered a man's plight. But there are an astonishing number of women who silently struggle with this vice. And I used to be one of them.

Even now, as I'm putting myself out there, I wonder what the fallout might be. There are people in my own family who don't even know about the abuse. And there are certainly many more who don't know about the addiction.

But I write this because I now carry an authority that comes from overcoming both, fully and completely.

This chapter is for those of you who, like me, felt that there was something off in their Christianity. Your faith is sincere, you genuinely love the Lord, and you want with all your heart to obey God and live the life that He has for you.

But something feels off. Something feels forced. And sometimes you wonder if you really *are saved* because you don't feel like a new creation at all. Too many Christians live a Romans 7:15 life; doing what we don't want to do and failing to do what our spirits desire. I struggled with that feeling the first seven years of my walk with God.

But in 2015, as everything was up in the air, and I was wondering what exactly my future held, the Lord used this time as the exact season to reach out to me and reveal that I could be as close to Him as I wanted to be.

There's something about weddings

It started with my friend's wedding. My best friend in college was finally getting married to her college sweetheart. They'd gotten engaged mere months after we all graduated. But it took them two years to save up for their wedding.

Miraculously, God sustained me and held me afloat, providing everything I needed to travel cross-country and serve as a bridesmaid during their ceremony. It was March and I was still waiting for the first royalty check from *Jane*. I was ecstatic to watch my beloved friends finally exchange vows and become one.

The wedding was beautiful and full of happy tears.

But in the days that followed their stunning ceremony, I found my heart aching with longing.

Longing for what I didn't have.

Longing for an intimacy that I didn't have.

One morning, during my quiet time, I sat in my bed and boldly asked the Lord, "If it is possible to be satisfied in you, if it is possible to be fulfilled relationally *by* you, then that's what I want. Please give me a desire for you that is even fiercer than this longing I feel to be married. Give me a desire for you that makes me pursue you relentlessly."

God answered that request so swiftly and thoroughly that it kind of knocked me off my feet. Within days of returning to Maryland, I found myself enraptured with the Lord. He gave me dreams, visions, and a deeper understanding of what it meant to be in relationship with Christ moment-by-moment.

Christ was no longer this nebulous savior whom I believed in for my salvation but didn't really know intimately. I was learning His character and understanding His personality. He suddenly became almost tangible to me. I could envision His expressions, the tone of His voice, His position in the room.

Coming from a conservative Christian college, I found myself a little nervous about this new development in my relationship with the Lord. Was it heresy to consider Jesus as being my spiritual husband? I knew the church was the bride of Christ, but was it okay to have that understanding in my personal relationship with the Lord? I was freaking out. I was scared. I didn't have a framework for this, and I knew that I was stepping into a more charismatic understanding of the Lord.

That scared me shitless.

Holy Spirit, Come

I remember when I first heard Hillsong's single, "Oceans."

If you want to pray a dangerous prayer, all you have to do is sing the bridge of that song. In it, the singer speaks about going so deep into the waters of faith that your feet can no longer touch the ground. Your trust is forced to have no borders, no boundaries. So deep, that the water pretty much overtakes you and you have to rely on the Lord to rise above it.

This all sounds nice on paper, but when God takes you seriously and receives that type of surrender, expect to see your life flipped upside down.

In a small sense, I felt like He was flipping the boat of my relationship with Him. I felt Him pushing me further and further into the waters of faith and trust as He acquainted me with a deeper intimacy with His Spirit.

I always believed in the gifts of the Holy Spirit. And I knew that the Holy Spirit was a person, and not just some random member of the Trinity. I experienced His conviction, His nudging, even His unilateral direction. But He was still a deep mystery to me. And I still had reservations regarding anything remotely charismatic or Pentecostal.

Too many crazies had given me the wrong impression.

But as the Lord took initiative, and began to give me

visions and dreams and prophetic words, I knew I had to step outside of my comfort zone. I started close to home. I reached out to a couple former professors who I knew were a little more charismatic than the majority of Biola faculty.

They guided me to speakers and teachers who had a very balanced view of embracing the Holy Spirit while also remaining committed to sound doctrine.

During my quiet time, the Lord encouraged me, "Michelle, you are seeking the Middle Road. You want the truth of My Spirit while maintaining sound doctrine. I will help you navigate this."

And he did.

He led me to a variety of "Middle Road" preachers. The most critical voice in this new journey of mine was a man named Terry Virgo, the founder of New Frontiers Church. The more I listened to him, the more he broke down Scripture, the more I realized that making room for the Holy Spirit and His gifts was essential to not only maintaining sound doctrine, but leading a victorious Christian life.

I also began studying the *One-Year Experiencing God's Presence* devotional by Chris Tiegreen.

What a delight it was to have the Lord personally escort me to specific dates in that devotional! It could be a sunny day in the middle of July and He would have me go to September 9th, just to speak to me about a specific matter that was on His heart and affected our journey in the present moment.

I never felt such growth, such understanding, such rich and peaceful communion with God.

It felt as if everything in my world was on the right axis, despite zero change in my circumstances. I was still waiting for a variety of matters to pan out. But I felt a level of fulfillment and joy that I didn't know was possible.

Easy breezy beautiful

… CoverGirl. Sorry. I couldn't resist.

You'll find that the deeper your connection is with the Lord, the easier it is for Him to whittle away at the things that do not match up with who He created you to be. During this special, sacred time of intimacy, the Lord gave me a supernatural love for Him and an ever-expanding peace that altered who I was. Things that would tip me into a rage no longer had power over me. Areas where I was decidedly weak, I found Him slowly strengthening.

It was as if He had been waiting for me to step back and let Him do the hard work of transforming me into His likeness. Since then, I never strive to be a "good Christian."

This is something He wants fully in His hands.

Choose to seek more

If any part of my story appeals to your heart, if there is any part of you that leaps up at the idea that you could be extremely close to God, I urge you to seek it for yourself. Run after Him with all you've got. What I learned in the season is that *there is always more*.

And the part of you that resides deep in your being,

screaming that there has to be more, is really prompting you to do what your spirit yearns to do. When you're hungry, your stomach will eventually protest on its own and growl. In the same way, when you're spiritually famished, there is a voice that rises up in you, telling you to go for more.

Your method of doing this can be vastly different from mine. But I urge you to do it from a place of expectation. Seek Him, whether it be in your quiet time, in books, his Word, or a new church community. And have the expectation that He is always willing to give you more— simply because there is always more to be had.

It is possible to live a life of deep intimacy and understanding with the Creator of the universe.

All you have to do is decide that you want it, and let Him know the same.

In my journey of fully going after God, engaging with the *personhood* of Christ, I learned a multitude of truths. That every single part of my life, big and small, matters to Him. Jesus is a steadfast companion—when you choose to be aware of His presence. It is okay to commune with the God of the universe in the moment-to-moment, because we were actually designed to do just that. And when you open your spirit to receive God and all of His gifts, He will always respond in turn.

Risk be damned

Following this path of seeking more with the Lord should come with the following disclaimer: be prepared to take risks.

Our God is an adventurous God. He's not reckless or careless, but He sure as hell isn't safe. As I began to wade into the deep waters of knowing His Spirit more intimately, growing closer to Him in the best way I knew how, He began to draw me out further and further into the deep waters of faith.

It started in the summer, when the Spirit placed a deep desire in my core to go on a sort of retreat. I thought of visiting the summer camp where I used to work, but then an opportunity came up on Facebook of all places. Terry Virgo, the man who helped me reconcile my burgeoning understanding of the Holy Spirit with my commitment to sound doctrine, was going to be in the States.

Based in the UK, he was visiting the church plants of the US during a weekend retreat in Massachusetts. I saw the invitation on Facebook and felt The Nudge. I bit the bullet and said, *What the hell?*

I reached out to the stateside church advertising the event.

"Hi, my name is Michelle Onuorah and you have no idea who I am because I am in no way affiliated with your church, but I follow you on Facebook because I love Terry Virgo and I really want to attend this retreat and meet him… but I have no money to do so and was wondering if you could help me make that happen…please?"

How audacious! How absolutely bold to ask this of complete strangers. Granted, they were my brothers and sisters in Christ, but they had no idea who I was or where I came from. And this is kind of how I knew it was from the Lord.

The same evening, I received a reply directly from the pastor.

"Hi Michelle, we would love for you to attend the retreat. If you can cover your plane flight, we will take care of the rest."

What?! On what planet does that happen? And yet, I wasn't surprised when I received that response. The Holy Spirit told me as soon as I sent the request that He would make sure it was satisfied.

I followed through with my balls of steel and took a flight to Boston, where I was picked up by women I'd never met in my life, and driven to Sturbridge, Massachusetts, where I roomed with another person I'd never met in my entire life.

Every single person on that retreat knew at least a handful of people in attendance.

I knew no one.

That said, the retreat was everything my soul needed and then some. It wasn't so much the teaching as it was the people I met, the times I had to myself, and the refreshment that comes when you're in a new environment. The Lord blessed me with the opportunity to meet several key members of the New Frontiers New Hampshire congregation.

I also got to meet Terry Virgo, who spent a generous amount of time with me, answering my questions, and praying over me to receive the baptism of the Holy Spirit. I left that trip knowing without a shadow of a doubt that I was filled with the Spirit and fully empowered to lead a lifestyle of victory in Him.

Unbeknownst to me at the time, this spontaneous retreat would end up defining the remainder of my year. All because of a lovely family whom God ordained me to meet.

CHAPTER SEVEN

Life is not a tightrope

How do you view life?

Prior to returning to the East Coast, I viewed life as a sort of tightrope. I thought that you had to follow God's leading and direction with precise obedience in order to remain blessed and lead the life that He intended you to lead. It never occurred to me until well into my twenties that God is far more flexible then we give Him credit for.

That it's okay to make a mistake. He's always willing to catch you.

In the fall of 2015, I received the final decision letter from Columbia University. Earlier that year, *again*, they wait-listed me for consideration. In September of that year, they let me know that it wasn't going to happen …again.

Oddly enough, the Lord had been working on my heart since my return from the retreat. More than anything, I wanted a fresh start. I was tired of living in the grad school decision purgatory that had become my existence for three years in a row.

I needed something to move on to. At this point, it didn't really matter what. I was determined to not spend another year of my life living with my mom, putting my life on hold, and living off of my dwindling royalties.

Towards the end of the summer, as I spent more and more time with the Lord, I begin to realize that I no longer desired Columbia University. It no longer had the hold on me that it used to. Around that time, I kept in touch with a lovely couple who had taken me under their wings during my time at the New Frontiers retreat. I'll call them Mr. and Mrs. Carter. The pair had nine children, all but one of them grown.

I got to know them, they got to know me, and it felt like a divine appointment of sorts. Mrs. Carter knew that I was waiting to hear back from Columbia. She also knew how much my life had been in stasis for the past three years.

During one of our catch-up talks, she casually threw out the invitation, "Michelle, if it doesn't work out with Columbia, please know that we would love to have you come visit us."

She and her husband had said the same briefly during the retreat. I shrugged it off as a courtesy expression. One of those, "You always have a place to stay with us if you're in town," type of deals. But Mrs. Carter quickly cleared up that misconception.

"We've taken in a variety of people for a few months at a time, especially if they're in the midst of transition. We just want you to know that you're welcome to stay with us for a few months to see if maybe God has something for you up here."

When I prayed about it the next morning, God's answer

was simple: "Go where you are invited."

Two days later, I received the rejection letter from Colombia.

"Mom? I'm moving to New Hampshire."

Discerning His will

So many things happened in New Hampshire, but I'll focus on the major takeaway from my brief time there.

In the two and a half months I lived with the Carters, I learned just how rigid I was in my understanding of God's direction versus my free will.

Maybe it was the failures.

Maybe it was the number of plans that had fallen through.

Maybe it was a deeply embedded desire to avoid getting hurt again by yet another failure.

Whatever it was, I no longer trusted myself or my instincts when it came to my future. I could no longer discern the decisions that I needed to make. I spent my time fully immersed in His Word, the New Frontiers community, and the beauty of my surroundings as I tried to painfully discern His leading. By the end of my time there, I wound myself so tightly in my efforts to understand His will that I fell headlong back into major depression.

Two key moments stand out to me while there.

The first was a vision that He gave me in prayer. He showed me a picture of the house that I stayed in at Martha's Vineyard the previous year. He showed me a table inside the house with numerous decorations littered about. It became clear in the vision that I had my choice of whatever decorations I wanted to use from what was made available to me. The house symbolized my life. The table and the decorations on it symbolized what God was putting before me, the boundaries that He established. He made it clear that within these boundaries, He was giving me the freedom to choose and decide where I wanted to go next. I already knew the answer.

For months, I had it on my heart to return to California. This desire became stronger and stronger the longer I stayed in New Hampshire, a state I never really came to like.

The second key moment occurred at the shore of a pond.

My host lived right near a private pond and I would take regular walks to the water, to be still and hear God's voice. As I stood at the edge of the pond, I sang "Oceans" to the Lord. In the aftermath of this praise, this anthem of surrender, I heard God say clearly and crisply, in a way that I hadn't heard Him speak in months: "Michelle, look at the water."

I did. It was rippling towards me in gentle waves. The wind and the current pulling it towards the shore.

He then said, "In the same way this water ripples toward you, *everything that has ever been a good fit in your life, I've brought to you.*"

Mic drop.

Mind blown.

And like a private screening of the movie of my life, the Lord gave me moment after moment of times when He brought about the perfect fit in my life. Biola University recruiting me. Every speaking invitation I never pursued but that somehow found me. Story ideas and unexpected resources. Jobs that I simply stumbled upon. The invitation to live in New Hampshire... Even the car I drove was the result of somebody *approaching me* to sell it. Truly, every single thing that had ever been a perfect fit for me was something that *He* brought about. I never saw my life so clearly.

He then reminded me of all the times I struggled and strove to achieve or acquire something. How it always failed; that even the goals I successfully went after were never a truly great fit—only the results *He* brought to me.

I'm not saying that this is the reality for everyone. There are Christians who need a kick in the pants. There are certainly believers who are weak in taking initiative and need God to help them have more pep in their step. But in this moment, on the pond, the Lord was revealing *to me* that *I* had always been a striver, when He had called me to be His child.

With these two visions in mind, I returned to Maryland with a made-up mind.

I was moving back to California.

Expect to be caught

December 2015 was one of the hardest months of my life.

I moved back to Maryland right before Thanksgiving, but instead of returning to my childhood home, I moved in with my aunt and uncle about an hour away. I learned that the foreclosure process on our home was actually going through this time. It looked like we were definitely losing the house this time. My mom, who has a faith of steel, still believed that the home could be saved by standing on the Word of God.

Looking back, I wish we had all believed right alongside her. After all, it was her faith and her declarations that had kept us in the house for five years without paying the mortgage.

This was an incredibly painful season—one that is difficult for me to recount even now.

Suffice it to say, we lost the house two weeks before Christmas and we moved everything out the night before the locks were changed. It was chaotic, stressful, and deeply, deeply hurtful. Maybe those five years in that home were five years of grace from God. The house was really on its last leg, after all.

Or maybe it was a home that He would have preserved for us had we kept on believing.

Either way, what was done was done.

Our home was gone.

In the midst of all this transition, I was worked frantically at "Operation: Return to California." I reached out to all of my college friends and contacts, asking for a place to stay until I could get a job and get on my own two feet.

Remember what I told you earlier about God's confirmation? Well, that confirmation came in the form of a dear friend, Judy. Out of nowhere, she and her husband generously offered me the guest room in their apartment.

Rent free. For as long as I needed it. Accommodations to make this move a reality.

His will, His bill

Friends, if God calls you to take a risk, expect Him to catch you.

When I told my family I was moving to California and crashing with friends, every last one of them thought I was crazy.

"What?!"

"Who are you staying with?"

"We don't have any family out there!"

"What if it doesn't work out with your friend?"

What if. What if. What if.

Up until this point, I'd lived my life full of what-ifs. By now, though, I knew that nothing was truly safe. That God nudges us in our desires; and when you say yes to Him, He is faithful to you.

This was the biggest risk I was ever going to take. But I knew that I knew that I knew that He would catch me—because I chose to throw the full weight of my lot into Him.

And catch me He did.

I shipped all of my belongings, including my car, to my friends and bought a one-way flight to California. Within five weeks of arriving in San Diego, I landed a full-time position at a respected investment firm. And true to form, this was a position that practically fell into my lap.

After striving from one job application to another, I told

the Lord I was sick and tired of the job hunt.

"Then stop hunting," He replied.

What?! I couldn't have heard Him right.

But no, I did.

"Stop job hunting," He repeated. "I'll bring you the right job."

That same afternoon, I received an email from my temp agent: "Hey, we have a full-time position in Del Mar for a receptionist. Can we submit your resume for the position?"

I moved out to San Diego two days before my twenty-fifth birthday. Five short weeks later, I was working in a full-time position with benefits.

A few months after that, I found a place to live.

It was as if I threw myself into the middle of the ocean and God made a raft appear.

It all comes down to trust.

Why would God challenge us to trust Him and take risks if He wasn't willing to catch us in the fall? Friend, don't be afraid to fall back into the loving arms of God. It's okay to feel fear, but it's not okay to live by it.

Ask the Lord and yourself if there is a risk He is challenging you to make. Get to the root of what is holding you back and choose to be ruthless with it.

When you live a life in which you expect God, your Perfect Father, to catch you, the sky is truly the limit.

CHAPTER EIGHT

Deal with your grief before it deals with you

I was a hot mess.

A full-blown, out-of-control, hot mess.

The thing about trauma is that after the first impact of the traumatic event, we have a tendency to shield ourselves, choosing not to think about it or dwell over it. Within the span of six months, I'd moved three times, experienced the loss of my childhood home, received yet another rejection from grad school, experienced the death of a dream, and at the start of 2016, the actual death of my younger cousin in a tragic car accident.

When I landed in San Diego, I was a mess. But because I had a mission to get a job and get on my feet as soon as humanly possible, I pushed past the pain of everything that happened and tried to block it out in order to survive. You can only do this for so long. And it is inevitable that when you hit another stressful situation, all of the pain that you've already endured will come rearing its ugly head back into the forefront.

My job at the investment firm quickly turned from a blessing into another burden.

And not the burden of a normal nine-to-five, with responsibilities and performance expectations—that I could handle. It was the burden of an office culture that was sneaky, underhanded, and downright toxic. Within days, I learned of the gossiping culture within the firm. If somebody had a problem with how I did things, they wouldn't tell me directly to my face or correct me in the moment…but they *would* go behind my back and complain to my manager.

During our weekly update meetings, I never knew what nasty surprise would await me, because for every bit of praise there was for my work, there was a veiled barb about how somebody else in the firm wanted something done differently. And of course, my manager never attributed the critique to any particular person, so it quickly became a Big Brother-esque atmosphere.

This would all be fine if the culture was just about tepidly complaining and moving on. But within my first month or two there, I saw a handful of employees get unceremoniously dismissed due to the exact culture I described. Prior to 2013, I always believed that if I did my best and worked with a spirit of excellence, I would remain invincible. But I knew now that the culture of an office could be just as lethal to one's employment as poor performance.

I was hired as a receptionist, but the job also included serving as an assistant marketing strategist, assistant event planner, head catering consultant, and office supply monitor and manager. And when I wasn't doing all of this on top of greeting clients, answering the phones, and managing the firm-wide calendar, I was also responsible for reconciling the reimbursements of all of the firm's senior management.

A position that was originally advertised as a receptionist totally focused on the client experience, quickly morphed into a jack-of-all-trades position.

Millennial Disclaimer: I am not a lazy human being. Millennials get such crap all the time for being entitled, lazy, uncommitted. I am not saying that our generation is without its faults. But part of the problem with this narrative is a.) who is to blame for the entitlement in a generation? The generation who raised them. And b.) at what point do Millennials have the right to express when something is wrong in their work environment?

I entered the position with the best of intentions and the hardest of work ethics. I came in early and often stayed late. But because I felt the accusations viciously attributed to my generation, I found it difficult to speak up for myself when I felt that things were off.

In the end, I rose to the challenge and within five months, received a raise. But that didn't change the fact that I was suffering from stomach problems due to the stress of the job. I had regular nightmares about not performing some task or being called *to task* by my manager. Every Monday, I entered the office, wondering if this would be the week that I was fired because of some unforeseen mistake I made or error that I hadn't been made aware of.

This type of stress would be strenuous for even the healthiest of adults. But here I was, with a history of clinical depression, which had reared its ugly head again, struggling to cope with the plethora of trauma that I'd experienced not only in the past year, but the two before it.

No one in that office knew just how dire my financial situation had been the previous year. No one knew about having to open a refrigerator that was nearly empty. No one knew about the water tank that died and flooded the basement and didn't allow us to have hot running water in the house. No one knew that after years of praying and working for a breakthrough, my family and I lost the home that my mother worked so hard to procure. And no one knew that just a month before being hired, I lost a beloved family member to a senseless car accident.

Every day, I walked in with that baggage on my shoulders and unwittingly, they added another boulder right on top of it.

To be fair, my co-workers didn't need to know what was going on or where I was coming from. It wasn't their responsibility. But it didn't change the fact that I was breaking under the pressure of it all, past trauma and present trial. I found myself quickly cracking up at the job. I would get things done early, if not right on time, but I found it difficult to shake off the plethora of nitpicking that my pedantic manager subjected me to.

Even though I grew accustomed to the neurotic culture of the office, I still struggled immensely with the backbiting and the lack of genuine connection between fellow human beings in the office setting. It blew my mind that the same person who would spend half an hour at my desk, chatting and laughing, sharing stories about themselves and their family, would so easily turn around and bitch about me to my manager, risking my job and my livelihood. I didn't know who to trust. And that made me feel incredibly insecure in the backdrop of an already unstable time in my life.

Chasing health

As soon as I landed a steady job, I did everything possible to take better care of myself since I now had the financial resources to do so. As soon as I was eligible, I saw a doctor for my physical health. I was underweight due to the stress of everything I endured, and special supplements were prescribed to me to get my calcium levels back up.

After sleeping on my aunt's couch for six weeks, and then my friends' air mattress for four months, my back was absolutely shredded. I found it difficult to remain seated at my desk in the office for eight hours. It felt like an elephant was standing on my back every single minute of those shifts. I saw a chiropractor and started getting adjusted, which helped me to start feeling like a normal human being again.

If only getting mental health care was as simple as walking into a random chiropractic office.

Through my insurance, I had access to Kaiser's mental health professionals. It was difficult to navigate due to my schedule, but I started seeing a therapist in the hopes that I could receive immediate attention for everything that had happened recently. But unlike chiropractic care, where all you really need is a specific set of adjustments, finding a mental health professional who is suited to your temperament and needs can be a long and arduous process.

I went from one therapist to another, one psychiatrist to another. Doing my best to get the help that I desperately needed, but failing to get it quickly enough. It was as if my grief was an avalanche threatening to overtake me; after outrunning it just enough to get a job to survive, Grief's Avalanche caught up with me and I found myself losing control of my emotional state. With every stressor at work, I felt myself questioning my decision to move back to California.

I had no family, only two friends, and I could feel myself slipping into the bowels of depression that I was so desperate to avoid for the past three years. Everything was stacked against me: work life, home life, the unending loneliness, health issues, and my inability to get the help I needed. During this period, I spent all my spare time attempting to get plugged into a variety of churches, firmly believing I would find community there. But I just could not secure the right fit.

There's something that eats at you when you put your best foot forward to change your life and you see next to nothing in the way of progress. I was determined to invest in myself, but for one reason or another, it was extremely difficult to get the help I needed in the time frame I needed it.

The body of Christ

Things became desperate with my mental situation, and I found myself having to lean hard on people I barely knew at a local church life group. I was reeling with thoughts of suicide, wondering when, where, and how I would take my life in a way that was most convenient for whoever found me. I didn't want to die, but I wanted the pain to end and having gone through clinical depression in college, I felt a deep sense of despair that I was relapsing.

In the end, the small community that I found in a church's life group probably saved my life.

They didn't have all the answers, but they did know to pray over me, prophesy to me, and encourage me that this wasn't the end of my story. They also helped me by researching a variety of affordable Christian therapists, eventually helping me connect with one at a local YMCA within my budget.

It helped to know that I now had someone I liked and trusted to consistently talk to each week about the daily stressors I was dealing with. On top of that, I finally received a prescription for antidepressants that further helped me stabilize my mood. I found that I was taking a more measured approach in my day-to-day living, and I was able to better control my emotional response to the never-ending crap at my job.

Over time, I began to surrender the things that I truly didn't have control over and found my health continued to improve.

Deal with your shit.

Trauma and stressors are an inevitable part of life. I remember as a teenager, believing that life was just one big obstacle course. I used to think that once you got past the obstacles, you would reach the Promised Land and things would be smooth and nice and fulfilling. And I still believe that there are promise lands of sorts.

Once Joseph got to the palace, he lived a fruitful and successful life for the rest of his life (Genesis 41). But he still had stressors. He still had crap to deal with. The fact that he was able to forgive the brothers who sold him into slavery speaks volumes of the healing he committed himself to. The pain was still there (Genesis 42:23-24), but he did not let it consume him (Genesis 45).

Friend, I want to urge you that it is okay to not be okay. There are times in your life when it feels like life is dealing you one death blow after another. One of the most helpful conversations I had in the midst of all my struggle was when the person listening to me stopped me and said, "Michelle? You have been through *a lot.* You have been through more trials than someone your age typically goes through. I don't know what God is using all of the struggles for, but it is okay to acknowledge that this is painful, unexpected, and extremely difficult to cope with."

Sometimes you need permission to acknowledge the pain.

And that really is the first step: acknowledging the pain. So that you can then begin to deal with it. And choose to not give up if you run into opposition in your quest to get well.

Had I totally given up and failed to reach out to local churches, therapists, and even friends for prayer, I probably would have lost my job by the end of the same year.

I cannot say that everything looked like a bed of roses by the end of the year, but for the first time, I found myself feeling stable and empowered to make real changes in my life. I'd received a healthy bonus from my job, I made new friends at a church the Lord serendipitously brought me to, and for the first time in months, I felt better able to look at the bigger picture of my life.

With that in mind, I began planning my escape from my stressful job and into a new career.

CHAPTER NINE

Life = Change

It started with Megyn Kelly.

Actually, it started with my regular commute to the office. Because I worked as a receptionist, I had to get there before most employees to open up the front office. I was driving along I-805, noting how foggy and dreary and depressing the weather was. And as I drove, I began praying to the Lord about my life. Things were getting better at work. I had learned the firm's way of doing things. But I was still unhappy and concerned; I was starting to feel resigned to this office being my lot in life.

And that was a sad thought.

I knew that I needed a change, but didn't know exactly what that change should be. Leave my job? I hadn't even been there a year. And what would I pursue if I left it? The last time I struck out to pursue a particular career path, I ended up falling flat on my face.

Sure, there were people who knew me as a writer—even my co-workers identified me as that. But I wasn't writing at the moment. After so much trauma and grief and struggle just to survive, the last thing I could think about was a story.

I hadn't written anything creative in over a year.

These were the thoughts that I carried with me as I commuted to work and back home, day in and day out. I was grown. I was doing the responsible adult thing. Working an honest job to make honest pay to barely get ahead. I was paying my student loans but at the rate I was paying them, it would probably take another twenty years to be debt-free. I appreciated the stability of a steady income, but that income wasn't nearly enough to form or meet any financial goals. I was doing my best to please my boss, but often at the expense of my health and well-being. I was dying inside, one little bit at a time. I needed to change. And the Lord knew I needed it too.

I'll never forget when, two-thirds of the way through my morning commute, the fog suddenly lifted.

All of a sudden, the sky was bright and blue, with the sun shining down, highlighting the beautiful San Diego hills. The view was so breathtaking that it startled me.

I clearly heard the Lord say, "Michelle, I am about to lift the fog off of your mind."

He knew I was operating on autopilot ever since stabilizing my mood. I was a little too comfortable and a little too complacent with my lot in life. After facing one challenge after another, it was much easier for me to just retreat with the little that I gained and ignore His call on my life for more.

Now insert Megyn Kelly

A couple of weeks after that drive, I was sitting at my desk and found myself oddly curious about Megyn Kelly. I didn't know much about the journalist. Though I was pretty apolitical at that point, my first impressions of this seemingly combative reporter were not that positive.

But I knew she was successful in her career, well-respected, and a wife and mother who seemingly had it all—all things I wanted for myself someday. So I looked her up, and I found myself increasingly intrigued by her story.

To this day, I can only attribute this curiosity to the Lord.

Normally, when I look someone up, I read a bit of their bio and move on. But for some reason, I felt gripped by this public figure and needed to know more. Behold my surprise when I reached the end of her Wikipedia page, only to discover that she was set to release her first memoir in just a few weeks.

Lord, what are you up to? What is going on here?

I began looking up several of her interviews on YouTube, as she was already promoting her book, *Settle for More*—a title I absolutely loved. I found myself gripped with her story as she described her career transition at the age of thirty.

After working as a successful corporate attorney, married to a doctor, she came to the realization that she was miserable with her life path and needed a serious change. Fast-forward fifteen years later, and she was happily married with three children and a booming career in a field she loved.

I'll never forget her saying, "I didn't know it was possible to be this happy."

Without reservation, I purchased the book the day it came out. And I found myself entranced with her story. It was as if God was using her story, her testimony, to encourage me that it was possible to change my life. I still remember sitting at my desk, praying about her story, and asking the Lord why He was using it to speak to me. I felt Him breaking down the misconceptions that the past three years had drilled into my heart.

"Michelle," He said. "It is perfectly okay to *want* to be successful. As long as you're not making success your god, I want you to flourish and I want you to lead a successful life."

He then told me, "Character first, success second. Both will come, but in that order."

I felt Him challenging me to dream again. "What would your version of her success look like?"

I had no desire to be a journalist, but I did desire to have a successful career as a businesswoman, as a publisher. And I longed to be happily married and, eventually, a present mother. I wanted to be debt-free with not only financial security, but financial affluence. I wanted a rich and satisfying life full of adventures and travel. I wanted so much more out of my relationships and my health.

I realized, as I wrote my heart's desires, that I was about to settle for less and God was calling me to settle for more. By the time I finished that book, I'd crafted a plan and made a decision. I would give the firm exactly one more year. I would save up, prepare and plan. And then—leave my job.

I would settle for more.

When God has other plans

2017 was a year of change.

I think I always believed deep inside that change was either initiated by man or an unnatural aberration that happened every now and then. As a child, I always looked for stability. I always sought some way to feel secure. As an adult, I sought this most frequently in money.

I would think to myself:

If I just had a stable nine-to-five, everything would be all right.

If I could just control the people around me and get them to behave the way I wanted them to, life would be just fine.

If I could just preemptively plan my reaction to every possible scenario, then I would still have control.

If you didn't know this already, let me tell you now: control is an illusion.

No one has control over their lives. No one has control over their future. As a millennial, I grew up under the impression—brainwashing—that I was the master of my own fate and in control of my own destiny.

LIES!

I learned, rather painfully, that the only thing I have control over is my reaction to what life throws my way.

I used to tell people that I hated change unless I initiated it. This is a telltale symptom of a control issue. For years, the Lord gently revealed to me just how much of a control freak I really was. He used the most random situations during my time as a camp counselor to show me how deeply embedded this stronghold was. He finally ripped off the last of the bandage when 2017 rolled around.

In that time, all three of my roommates moved out and were replaced by three new ones; there were several major position changes within the firm; and a friendship that I thought would last for life came to an unexpected and painful end.

By the grace of God, my mood remained stable and my support system was held intact...but that was about all that remained the same. God used these transitions to drive home the point that nothing would ever simply remain. That isn't how life works.

Maybe you're better adapted to life than I am. Maybe you've had an easier time adulting. But the lesson I learned in 2017 was that *change really is inevitable.* Not the change you initiate, not the change you desire, but *all* change, including and especially *unwelcome* change, is simply a facet of life.

When I'm tempted to hold fast to a friendship or a living situation or a job I really like, I have to remind myself that it is *all temporal.* Nothing stays the same. Gone are the days when people worked in the same company their entire lives or lived in the same house for fifty years.

The beauty and the downfall of our generation is our hypermobility. And this does not leave Christians unscathed. Every single thing in life is subject to change. The only One you can really hold on to, the only One you can really sink your teeth into, the only One who will never change on you—is God.

Cling to Him with all that is in you. Especially when the

throes of life wash you about like the sails of a storm-blown ship. In James 1, the author talks about not being tossed and turned like the waves of the sea. This is next to impossible if you have nothing to anchor you in this ever-changing world.

Friend, may I encourage you to seek your anchor in the only one who is steadfast? The eternal, immutable, everlasting God? It was God who helped me recover from the loss of that friendship. It was God who kept me sane as the firm changed their structure over and over *and over* again. It was God who counseled me in my living situation and provided three new roommates, without me having to search for a single one.

And it was God who reassured me in the middle of that year when…

Losing and gaining

"Did you have a good lunch?"

The question threw me. I knew this wasn't a meeting of pleasantries. Even her demeanor while asking the question was hostile. I'd always viewed Karen (not her actual name) as a misunderstood figure in the firm. With white hair and a stern demeanor, this grandmother refused to retire and ran a tight ship. Others referred to her as heartless, but she'd always been kind to me.

Until recently.

There had been tensions and frustrations most of the year since my previous manager retired. Multiple changes and difficulty adjusting had caused the office environment to become more tense than usual. Despite my issues with my previous manager, I could admit that she was a moderating force in the office, softening the edges of people's pride.

Now she was gone.

And apparently, so was I.

"The partners feel this isn't a good fit for you anymore."

Wow, I thought. I could read the writing on the wall the minute we walked into Karen's office, but I was still coming to terms with the timing of it all. So many things were shifting in my life. This was the one area for which I thought *I* could initiate the change in just a few more months.

But they beat me to it.

"Okay," I replied. "Can I ask what the cause of the termination is?"

Once more, they claimed they could not pinpoint an exact reason. But with the office changes, they felt it would better serve me to pursue my writing.

"We wish you all the best in your endeavors."

I raised a brow at that curious response. I hadn't expected a straight answer.

There's something about having faced a similar rodeo before. As I sat in her office, it felt like night and day from when my twenty-two-year-old self was getting sacked in LA.

"Okay," I replied nonchalantly. "What's next?"

Karen's dark brows shot up in surprise. I didn't know if she was expecting me to protest, cry or beg for another chance. It appeared that she'd never seen this level of composition before when letting someone go. But I wasn't just anyone.

I was a daughter of the Most High King.

I could face my performance at that firm with my head held high. And as I sat in that office, I felt God's peace wash over me. I somehow knew that I knew that I knew *this* was of the Lord's initiation. I felt a peace about leaving and even a thrill that I was through with them.

I went through the necessary process of disembarking from my toxic employment and left with my head held high—once again, no move-out box in sight. As I pulled out of their parking lot one last time, I felt as light as a feather and as free as a hummingbird.

I pulled up to the next stoplight and read the bumper of the truck in front of me. My mouth dropped.

It read: "BE NOT AFRAID."

I realized that this was just another change. Unexpected. Very early.

But all in all, good.

CHAPTER TEN

Know thyself

When I was twenty, I bought a pair of handcrafted earrings that had the phrase "Know Thyself" etched into the face of the jewelry. I loved the concept of knowing yourself and embracing who you were created to be. But as I look back on that time, I can freely admit that I didn't really know who I was or who I was made to be.

It wouldn't really come to me until I reached my late twenties. I knew things about myself, but I didn't know exactly who I was.

As believers, we are told to find our identity in Christ and Christ alone. But that always felt like a nebulous concept to me, even in Bible college. What does it mean to find your identity in Christ? What does it mean to embrace who you are through the lens of Jesus Christ?

When I lost my job in the summer of 2017, I immediately dove into seeking God's will. I knew that the termination, though early for me, was actually right on time for Him. The Lord told me shortly after I started that job that I was meant to leave it on the 17th of 2017. My plan was to send in my resignation on December 17, 2017, but I was let go on July 17, 2017. 7/17/17. There was something poetic about that date.

And as I spoke to friends of mine about the situation, one of them said something that was striking.

"Michelle, you intended to leave your job in December, but the Lord released you from it exactly five months before the date you planned. Did you know that the number five is the prophetic number of God's grace?"

I had no idea! But when she said that, something came alive in me. I knew that He was using that period, the remainder of that year, for something special.

Initially, I thought this was the Lord's cue for me to implement my plan, albeit early.

At the start of 2017, I planned to save $500 a month so that when I quit in December, after bonus time, I would have saved around $7,000, buying myself six months to get back to my business, MNO Media.

I wasn't yet in the place to write again, but my plan was to start publishing other authors with a similar vision and tone to my work. Literally the day after I lost my job, after I applied for unemployment benefits and Medicaid, I jumped right into executing my plan. I purchased new equipment, I started posting ads for writers, I even went about transferring my business license from the state of Maryland to California. I wasn't playing games. I stepped out, believing that the Lord wanted me to just go for it.

But what is it about our beliefs versus His actual intentions?

Because wouldn't you know it—I could not find decent writers. It's not that they were all terrible writers, but they simply didn't match the vision or the quality that I had for releasing work under my brand. Every day, I would sit at my desk, and it felt like I was bashing my head against a wall.

Make it a brick wall.

I was trying to gain headway through pure brick, and my skull was getting more and more tattered in the process. It's a pretty gruesome picture if you think about it, but that's how aggravated and frustrated I was. Finally, about a month into my efforts, I met with a dear friend who prayed and listened to the Lord with me. And during our quiet time with the Lord, He revealed his intentions for that season.

"I still desire to do a deeper work of healing in your life. There are things that are holding you back, that are gripping your heart and mind—that I desire for you to surrender to me. I want you to focus on receiving and being for now. I know this is so hard but come, rest, be and let me heal you deeper. The what, the how, the when, the specifics of your call, your work, your business, your ministry will come. I promise."

It was so interesting to me. It was clear that He was freeing me to do what I wanted to do. In His grace, He removed me from a toxic situation, but He was determined to bring about the result *His way*.

The same week that I was fired, I learned of a prayer

group at a church north of where I lived. It was a prophetic prayer group, and I went there three days after losing my job. Before I even revealed what I was going through, the leader of the group told me, "Michelle, as soon as you sat down, I looked at your purse, and the Lord told me He was about to fill it."

Now isn't that what every person would like to hear when they just lost their job? As the months progressed, I continued going to the weekly prayer group and eventually, I started going to their Sunday services. Soon, I started attending their regional events, becoming a familiar face in the congregation.

I didn't know exactly what the Lord was up to, but I had more than enough money saved and was receiving more than enough in unemployment benefits to do exactly what He told me to do in this season.

To stop striving and simply heal.

Identity matters

One of the pillars of my development during this time was learning about the importance of identity. It was as if God had brought me to that church specifically to have it drilled into me that in order to fulfill my destiny, I needed to have the right understanding of my identity.

I will never forget attending an event in which the speaker said, "You cannot reach your God-given purpose with a broken or misguided identity. You cannot fulfill your destiny with an inaccurate view of who you are."

Many times, we allow our circumstances and our pain to define who we are.

We see it all the time in victims of abuse. Unless they get healing for what they went through, they view themselves as worthless and they lead extremely crippled lives. In the same way, we all go through trauma that threatens to define who we are. The only way to maintain the true picture of who you are in Christ is to run after your healing, hold on to it, and embrace as well as rehearse the truth of who God says you are.

I used to think this meant finding a bunch of Scriptures in the Bible and reciting them over and over again. To a degree, that is part of it. I am the righteousness of God in Christ (2 Corinthians 5:21). I am a saint, not a sinner (Romans 1:7). I am forgiven (Romans 8:1).

But there were specific identity traits that God disclosed to me. He told me that I was bold. He told me that I was a leader. He told me that I was funny. He told me that He called me to be a writer and a speaker, a media figure, and to own my own business. He told me that He called me to be a wife and a present mother. He told me that I have a David anointing.

He pierced through the lies that I had unwittingly agreed with and replaced them with the truth:

That I am loved.

That I am seen.

That I am known.

That I am understood.

He pierced through the financial struggles and the

identity lies that I carried as a result of them. He reminded me that I am the head and not the tail; that I am above and not beneath (Deuteronomy 28:13). He reminded me that I was destined to flourish and abound financially. He even gave me specific figures of what my income and net worth would one day look like.

As He revealed these truths about who I was and what my destiny was, I was faithful to write them down and recite them every day consistently. It may sound like magic, but as I repeated to myself the promises of God and the truth of who I was in His eyes, my whole world began to open up. I walked taller in the truth. My spine stiffened with the reality of who I was. As challenges and doubts tried to assail me, I responded from the reality of who God said I was. And I found, bit by bit, experience by experience, that everything He said about me was true.

I was strong. I was bold.

Others did turn to me for strength and encouragement.

And I was incredibly creative.

Things that had brought me doubt and withered away at my spirit were being overhauled for the truth of God's abounding love, meaning, and purpose.

By October of that year, I was filled to the brim with God's hope and love and destiny.

Pouring out

When you reach that place of security and confidence in who God says you are, it is only natural to experience the call and the tug to turn that purpose outward. In the same way that a vase will overflow if filled with water beyond its capacity, we as believers are meant to be so filled with His truth and love that *we're* overflowing and we have to share it with the world.

I began to ponder what it was that God was calling me to. Clearly the publishing plan wasn't working. He changed my desires at that point so that I no longer wanted to publish other people's work. But I still wanted to do something creative that made an impact for Christ and also satisfied my business savvy. It was around this time that I started reading a book by Ivanka Trump called *Women Who Work.*

Regardless of your feelings towards her or her father, I found this book to be particularly meaningful and useful in this leg of my journey. At the start of the book, she talks about the importance of passion. She states that it is incredibly important to find what you are passionate about and use that as the foundation of whatever career you choose to pursue.

I began asking myself and the Lord, *What is it that I'm actually passionate about? What is it that you have made me passionate about, God? What have you put me on this Earth to do, and what would bring the most fulfillment to me as a vocation?*

I remember getting so worked up about finding the answer to this. I was lying on my bed, pouring out my heart to God about how important it was for me to find what I was passionate about. Hadn't He read Ivanka's book?!

Finally, in the quiet aftermath of my cries, the Lord

gently told me, "You are passionate about light."

That may seem like an odd choice of words but as soon as He said it, I knew exactly what He meant. After years of struggling with clinical depression, I was passionate about living life on the bright side. I found that when I watched shows or movies that had an enormous amount of light in them, literally, my spirit lifted.

The actual view of a bright setting brought life to my soul. And then the Lord revealed to me that I've always had a passion for learning what it meant to live my best life. Since childhood, I loved reading articles on health and wellness and taking better care of oneself.

I firmly believed, and still do, that we are placed on this Earth to not just survive but thrive. And as He revealed all of these traits to me, the vision for what He would have me do next sprang forth right before my eyes. I decided to create an online platform devoted to exploring what it meant to live life in God's light.

Over the next two months, I wrote, developed, shot and produced a web series called *Life in His Light*. It was produced and designed to help Christians who have struggled with depression, negative thinking, or skewed views of God. I never felt more alive in producing something. Writing was incredibly fulfilling, but never as fulfilling as this show. *Life in His Light* was finally the perfect combination of my experience, talent, education, and insight. It took my speaking gifts and combined them with my film education, enhancing this pairing with the trials that I'd endured and conquered.

Back to you

When you look in the mirror and see yourself, who do you see reflected?

Do you see someone worthy of love and affection? Do you see someone who is victorious, a winner? Or do you see someone who has been so battered by life, they're barely hanging on?

Whatever you see, I want you to challenge yourself to see who you are through the eyes of God. It's as simple as quieting yourself down and asking the Lord directly, "Who am I to you?"

Write down what He says without reservation, without arguing, and then look back on what He says and compare it to your perception. It is okay to then argue with Him about what He sees. Because in the process, He may just reveal to you the hang-ups and the hurt that need to be healed on your journey to the true realization of your identity.

When I decided to embrace who God said I was, I resolved to make that process as quick as possible. I was eager to move on with my life and step forward into the glorious future He had for me.

You do you.

You go as fast or as slow as you want to, but don't give up until you reach the other side of who He says you are. So many people nowadays talk about "owning your truth." But there is no such thing as *your truth* or *my truth* or *her truth*.

There is only *the truth*—God's truth. Because Jesus is the

truth, the way, and the life. Put all your identity eggs into His basket and watch your life flourish in a way you never thought possible.

I can't promise it'll be easy, but I can promise it will be worth it.

Conclusion

What do you do when God tells you to write a book about your experiences and the lessons you've learned along the way? Well, if you're anything like me, you dive right into it and try to start writing immediately. I attempted to write this book over a year ago. But I couldn't get the tone or the topic or the structure of it right. You have no idea how frustrating this is to someone who has written for a living.

But as God has been teaching me, everything has its own time and its own season.

This book was not supposed to be written in 2017. But by the end of 2018, the Lord kept poking me with it like an annoying toddler, demanding that I pay it the utmost attention. Maybe the delay was because He wanted me to focus on five full years of post-college life.

Five being the number of grace, maybe?

I cannot say that I have enjoyed these post-college years. I've had moments of joy, moments of revelation and moments of breathtaking growth. But all in all, those five years were extremely painful, frustrating, and confounding to me at the time. I guess that's why the Christian faith is really a 20/20 deal.

As you're going through the struggle, it's kind of like a roller coaster; you're gripping the bars for dear life. But then you get through it, you look back, and you tell yourself, *that wasn't as bad as I thought it was.*

My hope, and I believe God's purpose, is for every reader of this book to glean wisdom from the tumultuous years of this millennial Christian's post-college life. I really hope it serves that purpose. Because I declare and decree in faith...that I ain't going through that shit again.

God bless you and God keep us all.

The End.

Author's Note

Dear Friend:

Can I call you friend? I think after all I just shared with you, we're pretty much besties now. Thank you for taking the time to read this book.

Seriously. Thank you for taking the time to read my story.

If any part of it resonated with you, **please take the time to write a review and let me and other readers know what you thought of the book.** I do read the positive reviews and it encourages me to know that people outside of my SoCal bubble are being blessed by this work. Also, sharing is caring! Spread the word about this book – especially now that it's in audio. Your non-reader friends have no excuses when someone can read it to them.

Lastly, please connect directly with me. We're new besties after all.

Please visit my Pinterest-worthy site at www.mnomedia.com. There, you can explore a wealth of resources for going deeper into the things of God, including my webseries, *Life in His Light.* When I'm not travelling and speaking, I love to connect with my new friends on Facebook. Join me there and know that I do respond to every message I receive as of this writing: www.facebook.com/authormichelleonuorah. Finally, if you want to be notified of new releases, go to my website, www.mnomedia.com, and sign up for my email list (you'll get a nice little gift for doing so).

Look at all those ways for us to connect! I can't *wait* to meet you!!

Blessings and love,

Join The Movement

www.lifeinhislight.com

The MNO Media Challenge

Stories are powerful. If you liked this book and think that others would benefit from reading it, regardless of their background, please consider the MNO Media Challenge by:

1.) Writing a review on Amazon, Goodreads, and Barnes & Noble.

2.) Recommending it to people in your inner circle – family and friends.

3.) Purchasing copies of this book and other MNO Media titles as a gift for others.

4.) Inviting Michelle to speak at your church or event.

5.) Keeping in touch with Michelle to receive more resources.

Stories can impact lives and with your help, a bigger impact can be made. Thanks!

Acknowledgments

I would like to thank Judy Campbell-Smith, Meg Ebba, Sharyna Scott, and Patricia Nkwonta for serving as my beta readers. All of you were invaluable to the development of this book.

I also want to thank Rachel Hamel. The Word says a good friend sticks closer than a brother. You were a wonderful sister to me during this incredible trial as I wrote this book in your home. Thank you!

About the Author

Michelle N. Onuorah is the bestselling author of *Type N, Taking Names, Remember Me, Jane* and *Atlas Died. WTF, God?* is her debut non-fiction release. The daughter of Nigerian immigrants, Michelle grew up with a love of storytelling. At the tender age of thirteen, she wrote her first book, *Double Identity*, and self-published it the next year. For three years, she ran an independent magazine, *MNO*, and served as the main writer and editor-in-chief. Her writing has appeared in *Vestiges Literary Magazine, Avalon Literary Review*, and *Medium.com* among others.

A graduate of Biola University, Michelle is putting her film degree to use by producing a new teaching series under her company, MNO Media, LLC. The series, *Life in His Light*, is designed to help Christians who struggle with depression overcome it. Connect with Michelle at facebook.com/authormichelleonuorah. Those interested in being notified of her new releases can go to www.mnomedia.com/connect.

Check out these other titles by Michelle N. Onuorah:

Remember Me
Type N
Taking Names
Jane
Atlas Died

Get your copy today!